The Customer Experience Playbook

A practical guide for Customer Experience Leaders.

JONATHAN DANIELS

DEDICATION

To Angelique, Aliyah and Lucas.

CONTENTS

PART 2: THE CX CENTRIC PLAYBOOK

PART 3: TRANSFORMING WITH ICON

FOREWARD

Customer experience is a concept, discipline and profession that is still very much misunderstood around the world. Whilst an increasing number of businesses and those who run them like to talk about it, all too often the words fail to translate into anything that could be considered representative of the 'science' that sits behind the words. In his first book, Jonathan carefully and articulately paints an easy to digest picture of what the 'science' actually is, taking us through the true meaning of customer experience and customer centricity and what is actually required to deliver real, tangible transformative change.

As well as sharing his thoughts on theory and best practice, he shares some genuinely innovative ways to structure an approach to customer experience transformation – his ICON process is immensely interesting and a different way of thinking about managing transformation. This book is also extremely practical, with handy indications of role profiles and templates.

In a world where everyone has an opinion, especially when it comes to the subject of customer experience, it is important that those who specialise in the subject are able to share their interpretations of the 'science' and how it can be implemented. I am hugely grateful to Jonathan for sharing his specialism - both from his head and his heart – as he has created a book that will serve as an extremely useful guide and support to business leaders and customer experience practitioners alike long into the future.

Ian Golding.

INTRODUCTION

Whether you like it or not, your business is competing in the realm of customer experience. I will give you an example. Everyone knows Uber, the ride-sharing mobile application that has taken the taxi industry by storm. They are considered world-class innovators and are cited by many as a great example in books and speeches about digitisation. For a long time, many businesses have sought differentiation through digitisation. "Let's digitise the way we buy train tickets", "Let's digitise the way we order food at a restaurant". The story goes on and some businesses established a powerful competitive advantage in their industry by following this technique. Many start-ups completely revolutionised their industries. Don't get me wrong, there are still a few industries that are lagging in terms of the journey towards digitisation but it's safe to say, in the world where I'm living, we are already there. Digitisation is not offering the same competitive advantage than it once did. It has become an essential requirement.

Let's get back to the example of Uber. Last year I was sitting in my office in Brussels and I was planning the route to see a client. He said to me 'Don't choose Uber, go with Heetch, it's much better'. I downloaded the Heetch app, I booked a taxi, I arrived at my destination and I continued my day. It wasn't until that evening, when I had a moment to myself that it hit me. I had just substituted Uber's service with another, only from a recommendation. I hadn't even asked my friend why I should choose something else over Uber. I was quite a regular user of Uber up until that point, so I had no reason to change. I decided to speak to some of the local taxi drivers to investigate why some people seemed to be switching. It appeared that some pricing policies might sometimes work in the customer's favour with Heetch and also it was possible to pay by cash. Maybe this was the reason why my client recommended it to me?

There was nothing about the look and feel, or design of the Heetch app that was remarkably better than Uber's. They both filled the same need: to connect me with a nearby taxi as quickly as possible. My client had an overall better experience and so he recommended Heetch and I listened. At that point, I realised the power of focusing on Customer Experience and putting customers at the centre of what we do. Whether you are a large or small company, in this day and age, if you are not focused on the experience of your customers before you know it, they will all disappear.

For a long time, we have used the words' digitisation' and 'innovation' synonymously. If I ask you to name three innovative businesses, I'm pretty sure at least two of the three will be technology companies. For so long, organisations have invested time and energy focusing on internal processes and looking for efficiencies and innovations to reach their internal company objectives. In contrast, Customer Experience obtains power from its focus on the journey of the customer. Mapping the sequence of customer activities, understanding where your products and services fit within the bigger picture of their lives and pinpointing opportunities to improve it. These improvements may come in the form of a policy change, or better training, or a change to your business processes. Technology may not necessarily be the driver here.

More and more organisations are waking up to the power of investing in the experience they offer to their customers. To achieve this, these organisations need to transform to what is widely known as being 'Customer Centric' – this means putting customers at the centre of what they do. The transformation journey towards customer-centricity is never smooth or straight forward. I wrote this book for leaders of Customer-Centric Transformations; people who want to transform their organisations and put the experience of their customers high on their agendas. More and more organisations are employing Customer Experience Directors, Customer Success Directors, Chief Customer

Officers and other related job titles. I wrote this book as a much-needed practical guide to support leaders in our field.

Whether you are introducing the subject of Customer Experience to your organisation, or whether you are further down on your transformational journey, the CX CENTRIC playbook and the ICON process can be useful to you. The CX CENTRIC playbook is a lot different from other frameworks in the industry, mainly because it is very prescriptive. The clarity and detail offers leaders something tangible to measure their business against. Hence, we do our best not to use high-level conceptual terms; instead, we communicate clearly and in detail as much as possible. This means you can quickly dip in and out of specific sections as you see fit.

My objective is to share the customer-centric mindset and support leaders around the world with a framework they can stand on. Sometimes steering a transformation can be a lot like steering a ship, it can get rough out there! Yes, it would help if you had your compass and your map. But you also need to be able to recognise the signs, to avoid rough waters. And when you do hit a storm, you need knowledge of fundamental principles to get your organisation through in one piece. Hopefully, the CX CENTRIC framework can help you avoid these storms. And if you are already in a storm, maybe it just might give you what you need to make it through.

HOW THE BOOK IS STRUCTURED.

Part 1 of the book offers a brief overview of Customer Experience as well as the role of a Customer Experience Leader. The second part of the book gives an overview of CX CENTRIC, our playbook specially crafted for organisations seeking to become more customer-centric. CX CENTRIC presents the governance required for a customer-centric organisation: Founding Beliefs, Inputs, Roles, Events and Outputs. Finally, the third part of this book presents the ICON process, which supports organisations who seek to transform to become more customer-centric. This section includes many case studies from industry professionals.

Depending on your experience, there may be some

parts of this book which are more familiar than others. That's because I used well-established practices such as Agility and Business Change as the foundation of this framework. I've also ensured that there is enough detail in each chapter so that you can skip through and read the sections that are the most important to you and your company first.

PART 1
CX AND
LEADERSHIP

CUSTOMER EXPERIENCE AND CUSTOMER CENTRICITY

We begin this book with some definitions which were kindly provided by the Customer Experience Professionals Association (CXPA). Definitions are crucial in Customer Experience. When other professionals hear the words *Customer Experience*, they often form their interpretation and then go along with it! Part of your role as a leader is to set clear definitions and educate your peers on what we do. The CXPA has done well to standardise the language in our field. Hence we recommend using their descriptions as much as possible. I present the key definitions below.

Customer Experience (CX) refers to the perception that customers have of an organisation – one that is formed based on interactions across all touchpoints, people and technology over time.

CX Management (CXM) is the set of practices that an organisation employs to meet (or exceed) customers' expectations.

CX practitioners are the skilled professionals who work within their organisations to prioritise and champion customer-centric improvements.

So let's put this together. This book offers CX practitioners and business owners a practical guide to manage and improve the customer experience their organisation provides.

In 1998, Pine and Gilmore argued that service organisations would be able to gain a competitive advantage by focusing on delivering differentiated Customer Experiences. Today we see this being the case more than ever. We've seen a rise in the amount of subscription-based offers, enabling customers to cancel and switch to other suppliers easily. Many services are cheaper than they were 20 years ago, due to efficiencies that technology brings. Because of this price holds less power as a differentiator. The service industry has been modularised, which allows customers to compile different services together to meet their overall need. Technology has also enabled customers to be more expressive, sharing their experiences with current and potential customers. Today individual experiences can have massive implications on company perception and this affects the bottom line and share price. The sum of these factors means that the power of customers continues to increase, strengthening the case for CX investment.

BENEFITS OF INVESTING IN CUSTOMER EXPERIENCE

We all know examples of who we would consider as Customer-Centric organisations. And we have witnessed them grow, awarded with exceptional profits in recent years. The profitability of customer-centricity is not a new concept. In 2001 Coldwell conducted research on Customer Satisfaction, consisting of over 20,000 respondents across 40 countries. The results indicated that a "totally satisfied" customer contributes 2.6 times more revenue, in comparison to a "somewhat satisfied" customer. That's a lot of money to leave on the table! Is this really a surprise? Think of a restaurant that you would describe as 'totally satisfying', then imagine that there is a restaurant across the street that you would describe as offering a 'somewhat satisfying' experience. Given a choice, which restaurant are you likely to return to?

Many CX practitioners who are new to the game, seem to find it difficult to justify investment in CX. There is a perception that returns on investment are difficult to quantify. My advice – check out the statistics. Investing in Customer Experience is not just 'the right thing to do' for your customers, it's also the right thing to do for your business. Better customer experience increases customer loyalty, increases referrals, encourages advocacy and can help to differentiate your brand. These lead to more significant revenues and profitability for your business.

Forrester Research conducted a study in the US focusing on five sectors. They identified pairs of companies in these industries and compared their revenue growth rates with their experience scores. In four of the five sectors, we observe that the CX leader saw much higher growth than that of their competitor who did not invest in CX. In some cases, the difference in growth was immense; for instance, in the Telecommunications industry, the CX leader saw an increase of 35.4%, compared with the laggard who achieved 5.7%.

Increase Customer Loyalty

Customer Loyalty results in repeat customers. And repeat customers are the foundation for a sustainable business. Loyal customers may also stay with you even if it is cheaper to go elsewhere. A study from Harvard business review analysed data from two companies, both with revenue of over $1billion. One was a transaction-based business and the other was a subscription-based business. The results showed that customers who rated their experience as 1/10 were likely to remain a member for just over one year. In contrast, those who rated their experience as 10/10 continued to subscribe for another six years on average.

Increase in Referrals

Investing in customer experience permits you to offer something positive and memorable to your customers. Positive and memorable experiences are the backbone of customer referrals.

"Create a customer who creates a customer" Shiv Singh

According to a Nielsen survey of 29,000 consumers across 58 countries, 84% of people completely trust recommendations from family, friends and colleagues. Hence, referrals play a significant factor in the growth of your business. Referrals have traditionally been measured using the Net Promoter Score metric. Which asks: '*How likely are you to recommend our company to a colleague or friend?*'

TOP TIP

The trick is to give customers something to talk about. People don't talk about mediocre or run-of-the-mill experiences. They talk about experiences which are remarkable, memorable and worth mentioning.

Encourage Advocacy

Advocates are customers who recommend you publicly. These are generally customers who love what you offer and genuinely want to see your company grow. If managed and nurtured correctly, advocates can play a significant role in business growth. Advocates can be leveraged as a resource to help you grow your business. They lead you to a more substantial market share, more sales and more profitability. We refer to this group of people as '*Customers As a Service*' (CAAS). I present and further elaborate on this concept in the 'Customer as a resource' chapter.

Differentiate your brand

Many organisations are using Customer Experience as a way to gain a competitive advantage through differentiation and innovation. By spending more time understanding their customers, they can uncover valuable insights and uncover emerging needs. In today's society, we are living increasingly digital lives and person to person interaction is becoming rarer and rarer. It is becoming increasingly difficult to build and maintain strong relationships. Investing in customer experience often strengthens the emotional attachment a customer has with your brand, differentiating your business.

THE ROLE OF A CUSTOMER EXPERIENCE LEADER

A leader who has successfully introduced Customer Experience into their organisation will have transformed the mindset and culture. As a leader, your first step will be to communicate the customer's perception of the current experience, with existing colleagues. This is often an eye-opening discovery for many employees, as they are accustomed to solely focusing on their own 'job'. It would be best if you then coached your colleagues to create clarity on the experience that you want to give to your customers. We refer to this as the 'target experience'. You then promote the power of data and information as a resource to uncover opportunities to serve your customers better. And finally, you inspire and empower your employees to put the customer first. This change in mindset needs to be defined, clearly communicated and it needs to become ingrained into the way your organisation works.

A great deal of customer experience literature focuses on changing company culture. Leaders coach their teams, helping them shrug off counter-productive habits and replace them with new customer-centric practices. We all know the difficulty and self-discipline needed to form or break a habit. Lally et al. (2010) found that the average time for participants to create or lose a habit was 66 days and this included a range of between 18 and 254 days. In addition to this equation, some of your team members may disagree with the choice to implement a customer-centric strategy. After all, there are many companies who are still in business today, who do not put their customers first and who are still very profitable.

The transition to the customer-centric mindset must be managed and led by example. This is not a command and conquer exercise. Leaders must convince their employees and take them on the journey with them. This is achieved by encouraging the right behaviours and co-creating, as well as attracting, hiring and keeping the right talent.

The CX Leader must bridge the gap between objective information - data and insights – together with the subjective opinions of employees to achieve a CX Strategy that the organisation as a whole can buy in to. Hence, this strategy must be formed through collaboration. The CX strategy must align with the business objectives of the organisation. Put simply, if you aim to be the highest selling pizza shop, you need more than the best-tasting pizza – you need to offer the best experience. If you are offering a mediocre or poor experience, don't expect customers who rave about you and don't bank on them coming back.

Education is an essential factor in transforming your organisation's culture towards customer-centricity. Part of your mission as a Chief Customer Officer will be to introduce the concepts and benefits of customer experience to your organisation. You will also need to educate your organisation by co-creating and educating cross-functional representatives so that they can experience the value first hand. A robust training strategy and plan is crucial; your employees need to be supported with the right knowledge and skills to be able to affect change.

Hence, a CX leader must assess the training which is required. For instance, if your CX Strategy states that you want to deliver exceptional artistic experiences, you must ensure you have some creative staff with artistic talents to support you fulfilling this objective.

A CX leader spends time presenting the current experience internally within the organisation, on behalf of the customers. They focus on raising awareness about CX within their organisation and push for CX to be prioritised. Don't forget that other departments have their own priorities, so without a strong leader, the voice of the customer may not be heard. The absence of a leader who prioritises CX often results in a misalignment between customer needs and the offered experience. This is why certain organisations are confused as to why they provide high-quality products, but don't manage to sell them or obtain repeat customers.

Remember, training needs to be relevant to the audience and ongoing workshops and activities should support it. It's not a one-time 'tick in the box' exercise! Take time to ensure that it translates to something meaningful and precise for all the different groups of people in your organisation.

Finally, a customer experience leader must be able to propose a way of working that sets up the organisation for long term success. Customer Experience is not an initiative you can introduce and then forget. Nor is it an initiative that you can place in one department and hope it will spread naturally – siloed thinking can block this. The change must be managed. Hence, the CX Leader guides their organisation to develop and sustain more customer-centric ways of working. The leader must also ensure that everyone across the organisation knows what part they play in delivering the CX strategy. By setting up a clear structure for managing the

Customer Experience, CX leaders can ensure that the organisation continually offers an excellent and improving experience.

FINDING YOUR POSITION ON THE ORGANISATIONAL STRUCTURE

F or Customer Experience to be taken seriously, the CX leader must be taken seriously. Hence, a Customer Experience Leader should be positioned in line with all the other leaders of more traditional functions. In the past, CX has often been associated with marketing. Hence, there are many organisations which start their CX programme in the marketing department. This is not a problem in the short term, as the most important thing is to start from somewhere. But if your company is in this position right now, I would seriously consider taking actions to move the CX leader to report directly to the CEO. Otherwise, you run the risk of delivering an unbalanced experience. You also fail to send the right message to the rest of the organisation, as many will see CX as a marketing initiative. If Customer Centricity is genuinely your aim, there needs to be a direct line between the CX Leader and the CEO.

As mentioned, CX needs to be prioritised at the top level and needs to be supported by the entire leadership team. Part of your role as a CX Leader will be to educate and coach other heads of departments to apply changes to enable your business to be able to deliver the CX strategy. More about this in the next section.

INGREDIENTS OF A GREAT CX LEADER

Driven by Results

A CX leader is someone who is passionate about serving their customers and wants to provide the best experience, taking into account the resources available. Although empathy is a crucial trait, contrary to common belief, they are not 'fairies' or 'do-gooders' who want to make the world a better place. They are intense goal setters. They set and communicate clear objectives and coach teams to produce plans which deliver these objectives. And they spend time checking the results, modifying as needed to serve evolving business needs, following and living Japanese principle Genchi Genbutsu, which means 'Go and See'. This was made famous in 2001 by Toyota, who released it as part of their fourteen principles. This principle emphasises the importance of going out of your way to understand a problem first hand.

Driving results in the education sector

Marilyn Daley

Senior Teacher, Birmingham, UK

Marilyn is a senior secondary school teacher in Birmingham, UK. She has the objective of improving the school's exam results, but was told to avoid the traditional classroom experience.

Marilyn identified four prefects who were interested in different subjects and invited them to join her on her journey to transform the school's exam results. These prefects are in their final year at school and are keen to give something back to the school before they leave. She encouraged each of the pupils to use their interests to help children in the lower years learn by organising regular and exciting activities. Each prefect focused on one of the four areas below:

- *Science, Technology, Engineering and Maths - breaking stereotypes by focusing on female students.*

- *Drama and expression through theatrical movement*

- *Software development - coding applications*

- *English Language and Literature Club*

Although Marilyn's strong interpersonal and

communication skills are solid, it's her attention to goal setting and her consistency which sets her apart. Every two weeks without fail, she meets with each of the lead prefects. She asks:

- *How have you advertised your activities?*

- *How do you make sure you will get a good number of participants?*

- *What activities have you planned?*

- *How do you know that these activities will make a positive impact on the exam results for each participant?*

Marilyn then went on to support the prefects, showing them examples of how they can produce evaluation forms, helping them to advertise and giving general advice and guidance. She also offers them additional incentives, such as pizza parties and other tasty lunch options to strengthen their motivation further. After four months of running the programme, the school noticed an uplift in exam performance from pupils who have participated in the activities.

Analytical Skills

As you will see in later chapters, to offer great experiences, leaders must be able to drive insights from data and information. In today's competitive landscape, there are many organisations described as 'data-driven', that can leverage profits and value from customer data. Information on its own is not enough; it needs to be presented to the right people, at the right time, in the appropriate format. And those people need to have enough time to analyse and produce actionable insights. A CX leader must establish, manage and support processes to achieve this.

So a CX leader must be able to work with technology teams to ensure the right technology is in place, as well as with Business Intelligence teams to ensure that data is managed appropriately and presented clearly. They must be able to communicate insights convincingly and this is achieved through storytelling. They should be comfortable interpreting research so that solutions are rooted in Customer needs, as opposed to being applied to validate a perspective or company programme.

A Relationship Builder

An effective CX leader needs to build and nurture cross-departmental support, from the leadership team through to grassroots employees. This can only be achieved by building strong relationships. Influential leaders spend time understanding the plans and ambitions of other people to know how you can support them. Throughout your transformation, there will be plenty of issues that arise. A strong leader encourages transparent communication to resolve these problems collaboratively. They are proficient in orchestrating and promoting inclusion of cross-functional stakeholders to help define or co-create the solution.

Sometimes a CX leader will be demanding, ensuring that teams work together to achieve solutions. The CX Leader is part-teacher, part coach, understanding that engagement and building understanding helps build support. If people understand why they need to change and agree with the reasoning, they are more likely to apply themselves and support the programme. Sometimes participants need a bit of encouragement to leave their 'siloed' ways of thinking. They understand that if the customer experience is poor, it's bad for the whole business.

A Strong Communicator

As with any management role, communication is key. There are so many things that a CX leader must communicate: the CX Strategy, CX Horizon, CX philosophy ("the how"), information and insights, risks and issues, the list goes on. A strong CX leader must be a strong communicator. They understand that communication is a two-way exercise. Seek as much input as possible from colleagues. And also, they have the ability to constructively challenge and discuss concepts and beliefs related to CX as much as possible.

A shared understanding doesn't come overnight. It must be built through honest and frank conversation, which builds trust. A critical element of communication is the ability to listen. An effective CX Leader will listen intently and openly and they will ensure that participants believe their points of view are heard. Active listening also helps to understand where gaps and internal barriers reside, which should be used to improve their communication going forward.

A Real leader - Not a Manager

A CX Leader must be open and remain approachable. They must understand that spending the majority of time at their desk or in their office won't cut it. Collaboration is critical to sustainable success. They engage with people, challenge them and are able to accept criticism. They foster an inclusive environment bridging people across the organisation and creating an atmosphere of trust. Everyone in your organisation is on a journey – you included! You need to be clear on where the priorities are and be honest if you don't have solutions for them. You need to lead by example as talk can only get you so far. If you don't go and visit your customers, who will? If you don't challenge others, who will?

Managing a CX transformation is challenging. It takes time, requires patience and the ability to stay the course. There will be setbacks and it involves much effort. Hence, sometimes spirits will be down. A strong CX leader needs to keep people engaged, keep that energy fire burning, supporting and motivating the team in times of need. Tenacity, flexibility and emotional intelligence are key here. Courage is also vital. The CX Leader has to be comfortable collaboratively leading change and helping shift paradigms, articulating differing points of view across all levels of the organisation. A CX transformation requires commitment and alignment at all leadership levels. It's a team sport. The CX Leader will define clear goals, establish timelines, milestones, measures and above all, not assume they have all the answers. Continuously asking questions gets to the best answer.

Bringing Clarity of Purpose

Errol Lawson

Director, Emerge Leadership, UK

It is highly crucial to identify the unique purpose of your business. This can be done collaboratively with your employees. Today employees are asking: 'Who are we? What do we stand for? What is at the heart of what we do?' Leaders must bring clarity to organisations and stakeholders on their purpose. Leaders who do not bring clarity bring chaos. Leaders must monitor and manage the alignment of their employees to the purpose. Personal objectives should directly align with the organisation's objectives and the organisation's objectives must align with the goals of the customer.

It is essential to present the current reality of your organisation. What results are you currently achieving? How good is the experience that you are now offering to your customers? Ask critical questions, answer them honestly and share the answers with your team. Leaders need to then set a clear image of the destination along with clear timescales. The destination should include expected results and the outcomes of those expected results. Finally, a leader must have a clear plan of action to take their organisation to their destination.

The above extract highlights the importance of clarity of purpose coupled with a clear plan. In addition, the below example demonstrates the importance of 'walking the walk' and leading by example.

 **CASE STUDY**

Accountable and Accessible Leadership

John D. Hanson

Author of Wow your Customers! 7 Ways to World-Class Service

In one of my retail experiences, I worked for an excellent store manager. The results showed, with strong sales despite being a smaller store with access to fewer customers. Our customers would make the extra effort to come to our store because of the quality of our service. The discontinuity of service excellence across the brand showed itself at the larger branch. Despite having access to more customers and space for larger inventory, that store struggled to keep invested team members and grow its base of loyal, engaged customers. While adding quality team members is a large part of the recipe for service success, the most important aspect to continuity in quality comes from connected leadership that holds itself to the same standards it requires of the team. Years of work experience in a variety of career fields has proven this vital aspect to me, whether it was with small businesses or Fortune 500 corporations. Long-term success depends on accountable, accessible leadership.

Strong CX Knowledge

A CX Leader must have strong knowledge of customer experience principles, human-centred design principles, design thinking tools and techniques. They generally are curious, life-long learners and spend time keeping up to date with industry emulators and Customer Experience trends and practices to help strengthen and advance their organisation. The last thing you want is a 'know it all' who is not prepared to listen. The CX Leader will ask the right questions to get to the best solutions. They listen intently and learn from colleagues and encourage others to learn.

In today's fast-paced competitive environment organisations need to differentiate amidst the proliferation of offers available to the customer. They must be agile and must learn, evaluate and adapt regularly. Synthesising the Customer Experience across all touchpoints (online, in-store etc.) helps elevate Customer Loyalty. Customers who shop across channels spend 40-50% more. The return on investment is realised when the customer is placed at the centre to inform business decisions. Results are an outcome of doing it right.

DO I NEED A
FRAMEWORK?

A good customer experience transformation framework is built on best practice thinking and helping you avoid mistakes which are already well known in the field. They are a great starting point for your programme and can also be used midway through your programme as a means of evaluation. Using a well-known industry framework can help you gain credibility with stakeholders, as people generally take comfort in the fact that you are using an industry standard. Frameworks help typically to uncover and minimise risks on your programme and can also be used to help identify gaps in capability concerning Customer Experience.

Many organisations fail on their journey towards

customer-centricity by introducing isolated changes. Consistency is vital – and for an organisation to succeed in the long run, it must organise and standardise its Customer-Centric processes to ensure efficiency and to protect the experience. Many organisations fail to achieve the intended change as they are unable to manage the level of organisational change required. This is why we recommend using an established framework or process. The Operationalise step of the ICON process tackles this issue.

OVERVIEW OF CX CENTRIC AND ICON

There are two key models presented in this book. The first is CX CENTRIC, a playbook for Customer Experience Governance. The second is ICON, a process for managing a Customer Experience transformation. These two tools combine to best position your organisation to be able to reap the benefits of Customer Experience as mentioned in the opening chapters.

Although these tools and this book is primarily written for medium and large organisations, many small businesses and start-ups can also benefit from the strategies and practices mentioned.

CX CENTRIC is a playbook which leaders can use when designing their customer-centric operating model. It consists of five key elements:

- Founding beliefs
- Inputs
- Roles
- Events
- Outputs

ICON is a process which CX leaders can use to manage the transition to a customer centric way of working. It consists of four key elements:

- Initiate
- Co-Create
- Operationalise
- Nourish

Jonathan Daniels

INGREDIENTS OF CX CENTRIC AND ICON

Agility

Agile delivery initiated as an approach to software development and took its roots from Lean Thinking. Amongst other things, agile focuses on early and regular delivery of value to customers. And hence, its practices have now spread further than just software development. Over the years, Agile methods have helped to streamline delivery in many organisations. The principal benefits taken from Scrum Alliance include:

- Increased ability to manage changing priorities
- Better visibility into projects
- More alignment between business and IT
- Faster Time to market

In today's competitive and quickly changing landscape, organisations must be able to adapt and deliver fast. Agile practices help this to happen. We see Agility as a critical ingredient for any Customer Centric organisation and as a result, we have included elements from Agile practices in our guidelines.

While having many benefits, we believe that singularly implementing an Agile Framework can only take you so far. Agility needs to be directed. If we think about our business as a car, I believe we can learn a lot. It is great to own a car, especially if it is fast, comfortable and fuel-efficient. But what is equally important is being clear on where your destination is and the route that you want to take. With Agility, more and more organisations are now able to get to their goals quicker than ever before. This means that the competitive advantage rests in being able to choose that destination well and to ensure that everyone in the car is aware of it. This translates into the precision of a strong customer strategy, supported by a robust communications plan for your organisation.

We have adapted and built on the Scrum methodology to propose a framework which prioritises customer centricity above all else. We believe that the Scrum Framework is an excellent place to begin, but by itself, it is not very suitable for Customer Experience Transformations as it is very IT-focused. It also does not tackle many of the challenges specific to Customer Experience that I presented earlier.

Change Management

I have created many training courses for Customer Experience. In one of my classes, we offer and discuss concrete actions that organisations can take to become more customer-centric. I mapped these actions in a matrix to understand the following:

- Which actions are driven by IT?

- Which actions are driven by business?

- Which actions require organisation-wide change?

- Which actions require change on individual projects?

It became clear that Customer Experience Transformations are organisation-wide business transformations. Given this, Change Management is profoundly applicable in this area. Some may disagree and say that we are still primarily driven by technology. However, for a Customer-Centric Transformation, the power lies in starting with the Customer Journey, using information to extract the needs of the customer. Technology plays a crucial role in supporting us to reach this objective.

There are many challenges within a Customer Experience Transformation which are similar with other

Business Transformations. These include:

- Communicating a sense of urgency for change
- Destroying myths
- Creating a roadmap that key stakeholders buy into
- Avoiding overcharging departments with change
- Avoiding looking like all the other past organisational change initiatives that are often not well-received and considered wasteful by many employees
- Making sure departments are well-supported along the journey

The ICON process has taken some concepts from Change Management theory and practices. This ensures that the above issues are tackled head-on.

Specific Challenges of Customer Experience Implementations

When I meet a Customer Experience professional for the first time, I am always keen to understand the challenges they face. Through these conversations, it becomes evident that many problems consistently crop up. Customer Experience professionals need tools and techniques to help them tackle these challenges structurally, to maximise the chances of success and to minimise the chances of failure. The following challenges can be attributed as uniquely related to customer experience transformation programmes.

Proving Return on Investment Very Early

Most Customer Experience transformations have the challenge of having to prove Return on Investment very early. For practitioners who are experienced, this is more of an essential exercise as opposed to a scary challenge. However, for managers that are new to the game, this can be a daunting task, mainly because if this is not handled correctly, it is likely to lead to the client pulling the project. One piece of advice here: Voice of Employee and Voice of the Customers gives you a strong foundation of information to start with, to support early profitable customer investments.

Focusing too much on technology

Organisations forget that technology is only one aspect of the Customer Experience. In fact, technology usually refers to a specific topic, known as User Experience. There are many other elements of the Customer Experience that are not related to technology and that can make a real difference to your customers. On top of this, over-focusing on technology causes motivational problems for your team. How many times have you heard your team say 'not another CRM tool'?

Lack of a Structured Approach

Many companies find it challenging to understand where to start and how to build on what they started.

You can easily ask your employees how they can improve the CX, but when you have a list of over 200 suggestions, which items do you tackle first? Being a leader in any medium or large organisation is often about managing volume. There is information coming in from numerous sources and you've got to quickly work out where you personally need to invest your time. This remains true for your organisation. What improvements do you need to invest in, in order to see a return on investment? What processes do you have in place to protect your customer's experience? Some businesses obtain success in one or two departments, but then they struggle to scale this success across the organisation. Establishing strong governance is a critical success factor for customer experience transformations.

ACTIVITY

Review how your team currently makes decisions regarding activities it undertakes. Is there a transparent decision-making process? Is customer experience considered as part of the process? Consider documenting the process so that it can be adapted and communicated when required.

Building Customer-Centric Culture

So many external factors are affecting businesses in today's competitive environment. Companies are under more pressure than ever before. Lots of new technology and initiatives can sway organisations in their path to offering a persuasive customer experience. Hence a CX Leader must work hard to analyse the culture of the organisation, evaluating the level of customer-centricity. For many organisations, this will require a collective change in focus and behaviours. And this is not an easy task. Part of this also includes attracting, hiring and keeping the right employees that will help your organisation to grow and flourish.

The below is a great example from Olga Guseva, on measuring customer-centric culture.

CASE STUDY

Measuring Company Culture to help drive your CX Transformation

Olga Guseva

Founder of Integria Consult, Russia

Corporate culture works like a glue that keeps all people in the company united to achieve common goals, to stay strong when times are tough and to be more as a whole than a sum of elements. I've never met a leader that would deny the power of a customer centric corporate culture, but there's a huge gap that lies between understanding and really building and managing a culture where the customer is at the centre of everything the company does.

There are lots of tools that can help build better culture, make relationships between employees closer and sincerer, but there are really few that measure and develop the level of customer centricity of corporate culture. The link between commercial success and customer centricity have been deeply analysed by Dr. Linden Brown from MarketCulture – more than 10 years of profound academic research resulted in a simple and convenient tool called MRITM (Market Responsiveness Index) that "splits" such a diverse and complex concept into 8 "manageable" disciplines that describe different aspect of customer centricity of the company.

By measuring each discipline, comparing the results to other companies and collecting ideas from employees, the company can develop a fact-based and well-prioritized customer centric culture development plan that will cover all vital aspects of corporate culture that relate directly to commercial efficiency.

Here are the examples how strong and weak corporate customer culture could look like – the picture on the left (courtesy of MarketCulture) side represents the company with strong customer-centric culture that successfully empowers its staff and is especially strong at seeing and acting on external influence like political, environmental, economic and social factors. Such a company most likely would be able to adapt successfully and promptly to changing situations (like COVID challenge the world is facing now).

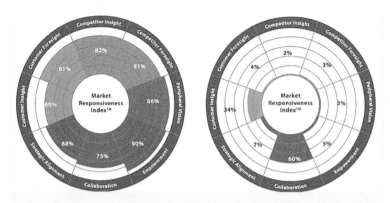

The picture on the right represents a company with overall weak corporate culture – while it has some ability to understand current customer needs and collaborate between departments, the company lacks the ability to understand competitors, external environment and future customer needs, it is also very weak on empowering people and bringing the understanding of the strategy across all staff levels.

The beauty of MRITM tool is in its simplicity and clarity – after running this research a company receives clear direction about where it should focus its time and efforts. This instrument is successful across the world – more than 400 companies have used the MRI globally. We've run a number of consulting projects using this methodology in Russia and can confirm that it really works, bringing clarity and direction in such a complex and important area as corporate culture.

Building and using insights

Technology, data, information and analysis need to be managed correctly to build customer knowledge and insights. With so many stakeholders and departments involved, this can quickly become a complicated process and hence needs to be managed effectively. This is discussed in more detail in the 'Inputs' section of CX CENTRIC.

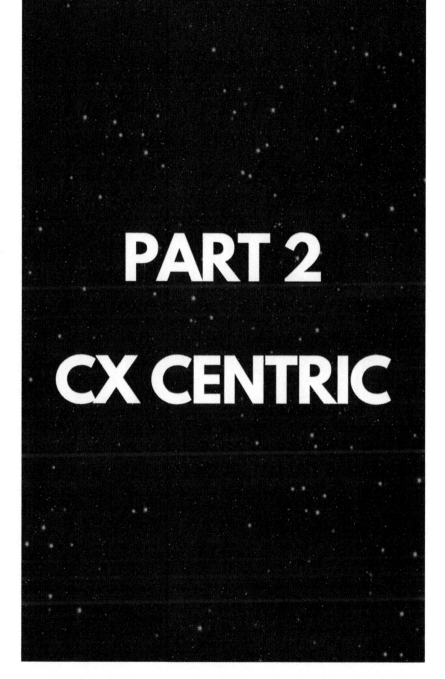

PART 2

CX CENTRIC

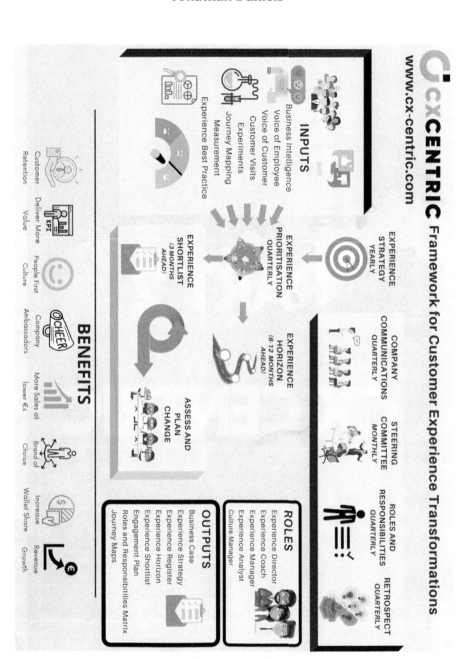

OUR FOUNDING BELIEFS

Shared Belief and Shared Problem

To benefit from customer loyalty and advocacy, your business needs to have a higher purpose and strong core values. This higher purpose is not about "doing good" for the world, but is actually about communicating a unifying vision for the business, its customers as well as other stakeholders. We recommend using the board of beliefs tool for this. List the views or values that underpin what your business stands for. It would help if you aim to be very clear and I encourage you to be bold in your statements. Your ideal customer should share these beliefs. Businesses who share a meaningful relationship with their Customers build company advocates.

Now you have a list of beliefs and values that your business can stand on, it is time to identify the shared problem. Some people believe that companies exist to solve problems for their customers. This used to be the case and often still is. But organisations that want to build Customer Advocacy realise that by solving problems *with* the customer and involving them in the solution, they can strengthen the relationship. This is why we use the term 'Shared Problem'. The board of beliefs enables you to translate a problem into something more specific for your customers. The below example shows how the needs of two different customer types differ when faced with the same problem: 'I need to buy a car'.

Group A

Belief: I always need luxury in my life. I deserve it.

Shared Problem: I need to buy a luxurious car.

Group B

*Belief: I need something spacious for
my family.*

*Shared Problem: I need a family-
friendly car.*

The critical point to take away is that you cannot please everyone, nor should you treat everyone the same. The target experiences that should be offered to group A and group B differ immensely. Therefore you must be clear on the exact shared problem that you are solving and focus on that.

REMEMBER

Remember, this is not a one-time activity. Over time problems change, customer-centric businesses remain close to their customers and can spot emerging needs, leading to a competitive advantage. It is good practice to go back and regularly review the shared problems and redefine them if necessary.

Have a discussion with your team about the shared problem your business aims to solve. Has this problem changed over the last 3-6 months?

Strategic Alignment of Customer Experience

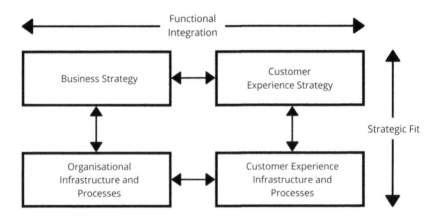

For many years, researchers have drawn attention to the importance of alignment between business and technology. Practitioners have invested much time focusing on how they can better align businesses strategies and IT strategies. They have also tried to ensure that their businesses operations are well-supported by its technology. In the age of the customer, this same principle must be applied to your CX

Department. In this section, we present two forms of alignment. Functional Integration, which measures the alignment of the business as a whole against the customer experience function. And then strategic fit, which measures the alignment between the operational capabilities with the CX Strategy.

Functional Integration

Functional Integration highlights the need for Customer Experience as a function, to align with the overall business strategy and operations. Business Strategy must be aligned to a Customer Experience Strategy. And Customer Experience infrastructure must align and co-exist with general organisational infrastructure and processes. This also involves challenging the alignment between how Customers view your business and how your employees view your business. A misalignment causes confusion and frustration for employees and leads to an inconsistent experience offered.

Strategic Fit

Strategic Fit highlights the need for your Business and Customer Strategy to be aligned with your Operations. Misalignment could be your business producing a strategy that it cannot deliver, because your structure and processes cannot support it. On the other hand, many organisations are selling themselves short. They have vast resources at their disposal but haven't formed a Customer Strategy. They therefore miss out on all the benefits that Customer Centricity brings.

There is a need to analyse and evaluate your Customer Strategy and your CX Operations as resources to be developed and supported. Without strong alignment to your business strategy, the impact that you can have on your customers will be limited. Over time as you acquire resources in this area, you are likely to gain a competitive advantage that is difficult to replicate by your competitors.

ACTIVITY

Have a discussion with your team about where your business is, concerning the four elements of the Customer Experience Alignment Model. Are you aligned? Which areas need improving? These gaps should be identified and formally picked up as part of the scope of your CX Transformation.

Customer-Centric Organisational Structure

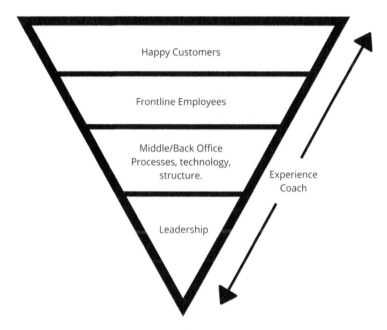

Gone are the days when leaders of organisations rule with an iron fist. The problems that businesses are trying to solve are getting more and more complicated. Businesses need employees who care and who offer their unique perspective on challenges. Businesses need employees who are 'vested' and who are proactive in their efforts to improve CX.

The structure of an organisation plays an important role in its ability to deliver strong experiences to customers. Many organisations in Silicon Valley have been influenced by 'start up' culture. This has spread beyond just North America. In offices all over the world, we are less and less surprised to find sofas, bean bags and Foosball tables. Silicon Valley start-ups are known for their agile decision-making, rapid prototyping and flat structures. This is a good basis to begin, but for Customer Centricity it needs to be taken a step further. We must challenge current norms in our organisations and guide conversation to always focus on to debate the value that they are offering for our customers.

We believe that applying participative management techniques coupled with the firm objective of becoming Customer Centric leads to strong growth for your business. Participative Leadership improves the sense of autonomy for your employees and increases their intrinsic motivation level.

Uwacu Révérien, Transport and Customs Manager, Belgium

"The true hallmark of participative management will be to create a collaborative environment and an atmosphere of trust and security, which make employees feel more involved and therefore open to taking risks and suggesting improvements. Without risks there will be no creativity, innovation or growth."

Gone are the days when sales people just sell. There are many sales people who state that if they do not believe in the product, they prefer not to take on the job. We have to develop how we view our organisations. In this model, directors spend more time setting and communicating the strategy and objectives for their organisation. Middle-management then work hard to ensure that the processes, structure and technology are able to support the organisation to achieve their objectives. Front-line employees who have direct relationships with customers play a key role in providing feedback and insights and helping to execute great customer experiences. Finally, a CX Coach can help an organisation transition to this structure and can also work with an organisation to help them leverage the most value from this structure.

CASE STUDY

Fostering a culture of collaboration in the Pharmaceutical sector.

Révérien Uwacu

Transport and Customs Manager, Belgium

Reverien is part of the Management of a European Distribution Site of one of the world largest pharmaceutical companies. He implemented collaborative leadership principles and practices within his team. He was able to build an atmosphere of trust and security, which made his team more open to take risks and suggest improvements to Customer Experience. In the period of the COVID-19 Crisis, there was generally a high rate of absenteeism. Without a department supervisor, employees in Reverien's team organised themselves, adapting their shifts to ensure that daily activities were completed as normal. Contractual KPIs have all been met and the customer is very happy.

Customer as a Service

Over the years so many businesses have benefited from implementing customer-centric strategies and practices. They have grown faithful and supportive communities of company advocates. These advocates are very profitable for your business and they are also willing to pay more, making up the core of your loyal customer base. But these advocates are not only there to refer customers and speak positively on your behalf. That is the minimum that they will do for you. Actually, these advocates can act as a resource for your company. If managed right, they can become a strong growth asset for your business. Some of the activities they do include:

- Acting as a sounding board for ideas

- Referring other potential customers

- Providing online reviews

- Helping with Beta Testing

- Product Launch support

- Supporting with customer service

Remember that company advocates need to be managed. They need someone to cultivate their desire to help and then to encourage and reward them. This is achieved through an engagement strategy and plan.

Leveraging value from promoters: Customers As a Service.

BlaBlaCar

Headquarters in France

BlaBlaCar is an innovative and successful long-distance ride-sharing platform which connects people who need to travel between cities with drivers who have empty seats. As of 2016, the platform had more than 40 million members across 22 countries. It's a very customer-centric company, starting with their slogan 'The member is the boss'. They refer to their customers as individual members of a broader community. And BlaBlaCar brings this community together. Over 80 percent of BlaBlaCars customers are satisfied or very satisfied with their overall experience. And so they have a lot of customer advocates.BlaBlaHelp is an online service run by BlaBlaCar's ambassadors. It allows new members to ask questions to BlablaCar's ambassadors via an online help mechanism. 95% of the requests received are answered within 10 seconds. Not only have they managed to save on internal resources by using their ambassadors to supplement their Customer Services team, they managed to deliver world-class levels of customer service to new customers.

Prioritising Customer Knowledge

I spent a large amount of the beginning of my career as a freelance Project Manager, managing both Organisational Transformation and IT Projects. As an IT Project manager, I was generally delivering software changes to improve products and sometimes to improve how large companies communicate and work together internally. As a business transformation manager, it was more about understanding the current ways of working and introducing new and improved practices to enable organisations to reach their objectives better. I usually worked for large household names and enjoyed my experience as an independent consultant.

Generally, an independent consultant has two goals above doing a good job:

- To be awarded with a contract extension

- To be awarded with a pay rise

Now to achieve these two objectives, people try all manners of things. However, the most important thing is to demonstrate that you are uniquely adding value. Often as a consultant in an organisation, you have a unique opportunity to show your skills, as you are present every day. Also, you have a unique opportunity to learn specific things about that company while on the job, which can give you a strong competitive advantage.

Many consultants gain their competitive advantage through knowledge of technology. For instance, there may be some Customer Relationship Management software in your place of work and you may decide to set yourself a challenge of learning all about the software. This way, when it needs improving or needs maintaining, you can fix things and offer relevant and valuable information. This also means that you can be very useful to other companies who use the same software. It's a good strategy and it has been serving many consultants well throughout the years.

A step forward from this is understanding the business. Some consultants walk into an organisation and after a few months, they can tell you exactly how that business makes money. They can tell you what each department does and specifically who carries out which activities. They can recount the key processes and how different people interact with these processes. They are even able to tell you the people in the organisation who you should go to when you have a problem that requires a quick resolution. This level of business knowledge is advantageous and can be used to offer insights as to how a company can gain efficiencies and can be used to 'make things happen' quicker than others in a large organisation. This value is hard to replicate as it takes time, effort and experience to gain.

A step forward from this is the concept of Customer

Knowledge. A consultant who invests the time to understand your customers in great detail is more valuable than someone with system expertise or general knowledge about your business. These types of consultants offer you insights to make better investment decisions. They are the type of consultants that cause nightmares if they leave and join a competitor.

One of the founding beliefs behind the CX CENTRIC framework is that Customer Knowledge is a powerful resource. The idea is that as the years go by, you learn more and more about your customers, being able to serve them better. Hence strengthening your relationship and keeping them happy and loyal. When your customer Knowledge is solid, it is difficult for competitors to come in and take your place. You can make better investment decisions than your competitors. You force competitors to compete on more basic factors such as product or price. I encourage you to position yourself to begin to soak up knowledge about Customers above all else.

Jonathan Daniels

CX CENTRIC INPUTS: DRIVING INSIGHTS

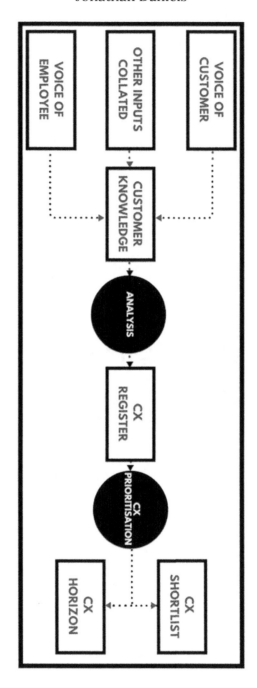

Anyone implementing a Customer Experience Programme should treat it like a science. This means that we list our hypotheses, we run experiments and we aim to be methodical in our practice. It also means that we do our best to base our decisions on evidence, rather than opinion.

This evidence needs to be evaluated and used to carry out further experiments to answer fundamental questions such as:

- What do our target customers want?

- What do our target customers think and feel about the current experience we offer?

- What actions can we take to improve the experience for my target customers?

The more good quality inputs your programme has, the more accurately you can predict the outputs of your actions. Inputs need to be identified and evaluated in terms of their usefulness. A person needs to be assigned for each Input and each assignee should have the same objective: To define the strategy which sets the direction and to improve the quality of data and information received for their respective Input.

For example, someone responsible for Business Intelligence should define a Business Intelligence strategy, which outlines the target Business Intelligence solution. They should then plan the appropriate tasks to deliver that strategy. While this may take months or even years to achieve, it will ensure that as your programme develops so too will the quality of the decisions you make. This, therefore, becomes a resource which your organisation can use to gain a competitive advantage.

There is a process that customer-centric organisations should follow to be efficient in CX Management, as shown by the diagram below.

Organisations begin by collating data and information from Voice of Customer and Voice of Experience processes, as well as other inputs. These form your basis of customer knowledge. CX Analysts review and analyse this Customer Knowledge and look to generate insights which are then added to the CX Register. Hence the CX Register contains a list of actionable insights which your business can undertake. The CX Register is then discussed in the CX Prioritisation session. The pressing items are distilled into the CX Shortlist (highlighting what needs to be delivered immediately) and the CX Horizon (highlighting actions which need to be carried out over the medium to longer-term). Research shows that more data, analysis and insights don't always lead to better CX. The process needs to be fine-tuned to better uncover the best investments for your customers.

In this section we present five tips for driving powerful customer insights.

Data, Data and Data

If you haven't already got a data strategy, then create one! If you haven't already put in place data governance, then this is something to add to your To-Do list now! The data is out there; your customers are carrying out many actions on your digital assets. You need to collect that data to find out how you can improve their experience. Things are moving very fast in this day and age and, customer's wants and needs are changing at a rapid rate. A Customer-Centric organisation needs to be supported by a customer-centric data strategy.

CASE STUDY

Measuring Company Culture to help drive your CX Transformation

Mandisa Makubalo

Unlimited Experiences, South Africa

The client was a not-for-profit, with the main purpose of influencing socio-economic transformation in South Africa in pursuit of social-economic justice, fairness and equality. At 44 years old the organization noticed a decline in both member retention and sales of new memberships. It was my job to change that.

We spent months doing qualitative and quantitative research, interviewing employees, members, sponsors and stakeholders to really see how people perceived them. Their website was one of the main challenges. It was really hard to see a succinct story. Different activities were communicated as if they were from separate organizations and they didn't appear to be under one umbrella.

The website had to be simplified. They wanted to quickly grab the user's attention and let them grasp who they were, why they do what they do, and what they offer. Hence we re-designed the website with that in mind.

Immediately we noticed they didn't have proper analytics set up. They needed to better understand who was coming to the site, how often they were coming on and what they were doing on the site.

The client had no way of tracking and scoring prospects so we also integrated a lead scoring capability. We set up a series of actions that would, combined with metrics, quantify a 'qualified' lead. We manually assigned point values to different actions that users executed on the site. Whether it was accessing the site in an email or via social link or download material, those actions were assigned positive values & if a user unsubscribes we assigned a negative value.

Thanks to this they can now distinguish between different customers based on how they interacted with our assets. We set the rule that contacts that scored over 30 points were considered as 'hot' leads and were passed to the sales team. So far the client has identified just over 200 qualified leads.

The result was a 40% increase in new contract signings.

Effective Management of Communication Channels

There are so many different channels that organisations can use to communicate with their customers. And there are so many different channels that customers like to use. Just because a channel is available doesn't mean that you should use it. Reduce the number of channels that you use and focus on delivering quality and relevant information. There is no point offering a chat service when you do not have the resource to support it; it just annoys customers! Don't forget that the aim is to provide a consistent CX across all your different channels.

Channel management

Tonja Pena

Principle Consultant @ Capital eXperience Group

If one of your channels is performing poorly, remove it, at least temporarily. Once you have data showing goals met on other channels, you can define success measures, tools and resources needed to support the closed channel, to decide if you should and can open it again.

Consider how well your business manages each of the available communication channels for your customers. Decide if the service you offer for each channel is good, average or below average. This is the basis to assess your strategy for managing customer communication channels.

Consider the Complete Customer Journey

When mapping customer journeys remember to start and end with the customer, not with your business. This same principle needs to be applied when you are building your insights strategy. There may be parts of the customer journey where your business is not involved with directly. What will you do here? Are you happy to take the risk and guess what happens? Or will you ask your customers for more information? To gain the maximum benefit from Journey Mapping, you need insights to supplement your primary research. This will help you uncover profitable opportunities to improve CX.

Please note, if this is the first time you have come across 'Customer Journeys', you can go to the CX CENTRIC Outputs section to learn more.

Focus on Driving Actions

Many organisations develop powerful insights about their customers but don't capitalise on these opportunities due to poor execution. All the information is there but the team is unorganised, the report doesn't get into the right hands or the information is just undervalued. A Customer Experience leader needs to ensure that there is clear responsibility and accountability for actions that are agreed, otherwise we are leaving money on the table!

Leverage available Technology

There is a lot of technology that can help identify how your customers feel after interacting with your touchpoints. There is also technology that exists to collate customer-specific information giving you a 360-degree view of your customer. Some technology can help you find customers who are searching for answers to the specific problem you are solving. Even if they are not searching for it directly. The point is that you must educate yourself on the available technology and test it for your customers. A great example can be seen next from GemSeek, who is a supplier of CX Software.

CASE STUDY

Strong ROI through use of CX-tech in the Healthcare Sector

Momchil Blaskov

GemSeek, Supplier of CX Technology

Our client, one of the largest not-for-profit healthcare providers in the United Kingdom, had set up a patient experience program. However the program was fragmented and most of the feedback methods were manual. This resulted in a lack of accountability and as well as a lack of real action being taken. The experience of the patients and hospital staff were both drastically under the set targets.

After creating a detailed roadmap, we made a quick implementation of the GemSeek CX platform. This mirrored the hospital's complex organisational structure, involving over 100 sites. All hospital employees received actionable insights relevant to their role. For example, the managers would receive immediate feedback after a patient visit, highlisting things like cleanliness and also the friendliness of the staff. They were able to evaluate the information and agree the next steps, whether it be training, or just communicating to staff to remind them of what 'good service' looked like. This led to a 5% increase in revenue, a 15% increase in patient satisfaction, as well as a 300% return on the initial investment.

CX CENTRIC EVENTS: RELEVANT AND REGULAR MEETINGS

I n this section, we introduce the key meetings required as part of the implementation of CX CENTRIC governance.

The events section of the playbook presents the required recurring meetings which we recommend to make your programme a success. The strategic organisation of regular meetings is crucial. So many people complain about not having enough time to do their actual 'work' these days. Many spend the majority of their days in meetings. More and more 'emergency' meetings are booked in at the last minute. All this causes chaos. The CX CENTRIC playbook presents a list of regular meetings which you should consider. Having this list upfront allows you to pick and choose and to plan ahead.

For each meeting, we present the purpose, frequency and our recommendation as to who should attend.

With great inputs and a robust process, you can achieve significant results. Take time to understand the current regular meetings that occur in your organisation. It may be that you can adapt some of these existing meetings, or maybe they already solve the same purpose as some of the CX CENTRIC events? An example of this is at one of my previous clients. They were a very 'agile' team and ran regular retrospect meetings. I adapted the retrospective meetings so that participants asked themselves: "*How have we impacted the Customer's Experience over the last month?*" This small but strategic change encouraged the participants to begin to think about their impact on the customer.

Finally take time to review the effectiveness and efficiency of your events during a retrospective session, with a firm commitment to take actions to improve the process. Remember that nothing should ever be final. There will always be ways to improve how you work within your team.

TOP TIP

If the key people are not present at these meetings, the decision-making can be slowed down and in turn, jeopardise the success of your programme. Give yourself the best chance of success by identifying the key attendees and sending the invitations out as early as possible. Work hard to ensure that everyone is crystal clear on the purpose of each event. Avoid running these events in an ad-hoc fashion.

Jonathan Daniels

Experience Strategy

Purpose: To define the target experience for your customers, aligning to your corporate objectives.

Frequency: Yearly

Attendees:

- CX Director
- CX Coach
- Culture Manager
- CX Manager
- CX Analyst
- Key contacts from across your organisation

To learn more about the details of the Experience Strategy, please refer to the Outputs section.

Roles and Responsibilities

Purpose: To define and update the roles and responsibilities matrix

Frequency: Quarterly

Attendees: Everyone involved in the delivery over the next 3-6 months.

To learn more about the details of the roles and responsibilities matrix, please refer to the Outputs section.

CX Company Wide Communications

Purpose: An organisation-wide update and commitment to customer-Centricity.

Frequency Quarterly

Attendees: Full organisation

To learn more about this, please refer to the Outputs section.

CX Prioritisation

Purpose: The CX Prioritisation meeting is where you decide on the investments that your organisation should make, in both the short term and the long term. In essence, we are asking: *"What actions will provide the most return on investment, in terms of improvement to the customer experience as well as achieving our corporate objectives?"*

The CX Prioritisation session is a vital part in the CX CENTRIC framework, because it ensures that your organisation spends time upfront reviewing summaries of insights and opportunities, to make the right investments for your customers and for your business.

In this meeting, the team reviews the items in the CX Register and produces or updates both the CX Shortlist and the Experience Horizon.

Frequency: We recommend that the CX Prioritisation takes place every quarter. However, in practice, you will need to find the right balance for your organisation. If the cadence is too long, then you will lose on your Agility factor and will likely be out of touch with your customers. If the rhythm is too short, you may be setting an unrealistic target for the team, which will be demotivating. We recommend that you set a cadence then review it during the retrospective session.

Attendees:

- CX Director

- CX Coach

- Culture Manager

- CX Manager

- CX Analyst

- Other CX supporters from across the organisation

Roadmap and Shortlist Planning and Assessment

Purpose: Once your CX Shortlist is defined, your team will be very excited to get into solution mode and start delivering. Before this occurs, there is a critical step required. This is the step that ensures that the impact of the changes on different departments has been assessed. And the next stage will be to work with teams to identify appropriate actions to minimise the impact.

In this meeting, the output will be the completion of the Change Assessment and Plan document. This is explored further in the 'Outputs' section.

Frequency: This should be carried out just after the CX Prioritisation Roadmap has been produced. And then additional meetings may be required to follow up on the actions.

Attendees:

- CX Director
- CX Coach
- Culture Manager
- CX Manager
- CX Analyst
- Department Representatives

Experience Steering Board

Purpose: The Experience Steering Board is taken from traditional Project Management methodology. The senior managers in your company must understand the status of ongoing activities and give feedback and support. Hence the Experience Steering Board is an opportunity for you as a Customer Experience Leader to present the insights, opportunities and results. Demonstrating how you impact customer KPIs, as well as organisational KPIs, will increase Senior Management support and confidence in your transformation programme. While on any transformation programme, there will be some challenging times. This is your chance to air out any challenges and formally seek the support of your Senior Management.

Frequency: We recommend that this takes place on a monthly basis. Again, we need to find the right balance. Too frequent and it may get in the way of the progress of the programme. However, you must hold the meeting frequently enough to keep your senior management informed and give them opportunities to input at and participate where necessary.

Attendees:

- CX Director
- CX Coach
- CX Manager
- Sponsor
- Stakeholders

CX Retrospect

"Feedback is the breakfast of champions." —Ken Blanchard

Purpose: The CX Retrospect is taken from the Agile school of thought. It formally gives the team time to reflect on the current situation and is an opportunity for everyone to suggest and agree on improvements to the current way of working. Leading a Customer Experience transformation is an art as well as a science. Things must be tweaked. We must be open to experiment. And we must be open to listen to others in our team.

The output of this meeting is a list of items to

improve the way we are currently working. This list will be added to the CX Register. At the end of the meeting you should agree which items you will implement over the next three months. These are then populated into the CX Shortlist.

Frequency: Quarterly

Attendees:

- CX Director
- CX Coach
- Culture Manager
- CX Manager
- CX Analyst
- Other directors

CX CENTRIC TEAMS

This section of the framework presents the key roles that we recommend for a Customer Experience team. It is essential to have a named person against each of the defined roles and to also review this list of roles and responsibilities at regular intervals throughout your programme. Do not assume that because someone is a culture manager, they should always pick up the communications tasks.

Remember that although organisations may use job titles which are well known across an industry, the expectations, skills and activities of this person may significantly vary from what you assume. In addition to this, the involvement of individual people can evolve over time. You may have one person taking the lead in the definition of the Experience Strategy. Still, when the time comes to update the strategy the following year, they have other priorities and are focused elsewhere. It is imperative to double-check who is carrying out the tasks, to make sure they are getting the support that they need and also to ensure clear accountability for results.

In this section we present five key roles: CX Director, CX Manager, CX Analyst, Culture Manager and CX Coach.

CX Director

Job Tasks

- Align business goals with customer-focused culture

- Articulate the operating plan, investments and tactics for programmatic components of the CX strategy

- Communicate and engage employees at all levels of the organization in the elements of the CX strategy

- Define a customer experience strategy that describes the intended customer experience, its linkage to overall corporate objectives and its alignment with the organization's brand values and attributes

- Develop experience principles and specific employee behaviours and interactions that reflect brand values and organizational mission

- Embed customer experience impact as a criterion for all business and investment decisions

- Identify key CX metrics for tracking experience quality, satisfaction and loyalty

Knowledge of

- Appropriately qualified in CX CENTRIC and ICON practices

- Associate engagement

- Business strategy frameworks and planning

- CX best practices across industries

- Strategies to communicate metrics and ROI with employee and stakeholder groups

Skills and Attributes

- Ability to assess effectiveness of metrics platform design

- Ability to create measurement strategy in support of broader CX strategy

- Ability to drive executive support and engagement in CX metrics and results

- Ability to engage executive suite in CX strategy design and execution

- Ability to illustrate ROI of CX investments

- Ability to quantify business value and ROI of investing in customer experience

- Ability to translate corporate strategy into well-defined customer experience strategies and programmatic efforts

CX Manager

Job Tasks

- Establish and follow a well-defined design process each time an experience is created or changed

- Identify interdependencies across people, process and technology that impact design of the customer experience

- Introduce new processes and tools to improve customer experience

- Maintain a dedicated list of top customer experience improvements, including which senior executive is accountable for resolution

- Work across departments and organizations to improve customer experience

Knowledge of

- Appropriately qualified in CX CENTRIC and ICON practices

- CCXP qualified

- Collaboration and relationship management practices

- Customer experience management dashboards

- Leadership and change management

- Prioritization process

- Process improvement methodologies and discipline

- Process management

- Project management principles

- Strategy and planning for cross-business-unit efforts to support the organization's CX strategy

Skills and Attributes

- Ability to drive action and execution of key CX improvements

- Ability to lead cross-functional efforts

- Ability to plan, implement and manage change

- Ability to translate data into clear communication of results, progress and actions

- Collaboration, influencing and relationship skills

Culture Manager

Job Tasks

- Collect and share stories of CX excellence at your company

- Develop and deliver ongoing CX interaction training to employees

- Develop communication strategies and tactics to share the importance of CX with employees, customers and the company

- Drive employee engagement and involvement –

from the front lines to the executive suite

- Regularly review CX metrics and feedback at all levels of the organization

Knowledge of

- Appropriately qualified in CX CENTRIC and ICON practices

- Best practices for cultivating a customer-focused culture

- Employee engagement strategies

- Employee hiring, training and coaching

- Internal and external marketing, promotion and communications

- Internal marketing and communications

- Reward and recognition strategies

Skills and Attributes

- Ability to align employee behaviour with customer-focused culture

- Ability to clearly communicate the importance of the customer experience strategy to deliver the organization's business goals

- Ability to communicate the importance of customer experience and corresponding strategy

- Ability to engage "hearts and minds" of an organization across employee groups

- Ability to take branded experience strategy and engage all functional business areas (product, marketing, operations, etc.) in creation of action plans

- Problem solving skills

- Relationship building skills

CX Analyst

Job Tasks

- Analyse and interpret results to derive customer insights and performance trends

- Analyse VOC feedback drawn across sources to identify customer pain points and opportunities to improve and differentiate

- Assess, document, track and report resolution of experience gaps across touch points

- Collect unsolicited experience feedback from customers (by mining calls, web data, emails, etc.)

- Design and implement voice of customer programs (solicited through surveys, focus groups, communities, etc.)

- Develop framework and linkage of improved experiences to business outcomes (growth, attrition, profitability, etc.)

- Develop infrastructure and mechanisms to capture CX data (surveys, operational data, customer behaviour, word of mouth, financial performance, etc.)

- Identify and map major customer touchpoints in the customer experience

- Report results, insights and recommended actions to improve

- Use customer insights to define and prioritize experience requirements and opportunities for improvement

- Use iterative ideation and prototyping (e.g., design thinking) to engage customers and employees in the co-creation of enhanced or innovative experiences

- Use journey mapping to improve most relevant moments of truth

Knowledge of

- Appropriately qualified in CX CENTRIC and ICON practices

- Customer journey mapping and touchpoint analysis

- CX data mining and analysis

- Design thinking and customer co-creation approaches

- Development of "branded" customer experiences

- Different approaches to measuring customer experience (e.g. Net Promoter, Satisfaction, etc.)

- Experience measurement and research methodologies

- Impact of experience changes on loyalty and business performance across customer groups
- Net Promoter score and methodology
- Qualitative and quantitative research methods
- Relationship and financial metrics (cross-sell, product penetration, etc.)
- Touchpoint mapping
- VOC analytical tools and methodologies

Skills and Attributes

- Ability to accurately map and depict customer touch points
- Ability to analyze and redesign processes
- Ability to conduct experience gap analysis and prioritize recommended improvements
- Ability to conduct predictive analysis
- Ability to conduct root cause analysis
- Ability to drive customer centered design and innovation
- Ability to identify key moments of truth affecting customer perceptions
- Ability to recommend initiatives based on customer experience data
- Ability to report CX data to different audiences in an understandable manner

CX Coach

Job Tasks

- Coach the teams on the CX CENTRIC playbook

- Coach the team on the ICON process

- Train the team on general Customer Experience processes and practices

- Train the team on the practices related to CX CENTRIC and ICON

- Integrate CX processes with the organisation's existing processes

- Encourage employee and stakeholder buy in

- Support the transition to the CXCENTRIC structure

- Facilitate the team to manage their roles and responsibilities matrix

- Facilitate the team to conduct an impact assessment after selecting the configuration of CX CENTRIC that will be adopted

- Co-create a plan for the CX transformation with other team members

- Work closely with the CX Director to ensure that the transformation objectives are agreed

- Coach the team to produce a customer centric data strategy

- Support the CX Director to develop and strengthen important relationships across the business

- Stay regularly up to date regarding best practices within Customer Experience

Knowledge of

- CCXP qualified

- Appropriately qualified in CX CENTRIC and ICON practices

- Coaching techniques and practices

- Co-creation techniques and practices

- Change Management principles and practices

- Agile methodologies and techniques

- Project Management methodologies

Skills and Attributes

- Strong communication and problem-solving skills

- Interpersonal skills and patience

- Strong understanding of the CX CENTRIC playbook

- Strong understanding of the CX CENTRIC process

- Ability to deal with complex and challenging situations and behaviours

- Demonstrate a passion for Customer-Centricity and Customer Experience

- Be a pro-active and self-motivated individual

- Excellent leadership and management skills

CX CENTRIC OUTPUTS

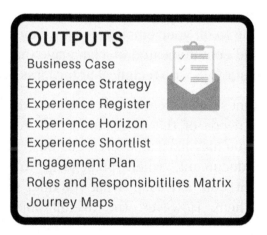

OUTPUTS
Business Case
Experience Strategy
Experience Register
Experience Horizon
Experience Shortlist
Engagement Plan
Roles and Responsibitilies Matrix
Journey Maps

As Customer Experience professionals, we are intellectuals. We need to communicate and exchange ideas. We must discuss and create a shared understanding of abstract concepts such as the beliefs and values which underpin our business. These concepts need to be translated into concrete and clear experiences. We then need to define and communicate shared objectives and goals. This is not a 'one-time' activity. These are tasks which need to happen regularly and need to be carried out thoroughly.

Outputs play a crucial role in helping to document a shared understanding of your CX. Although we specify a responsible author for each Output, in reality, they should never be completed in isolation. All Outputs should be created collaboratively drawing from departments across the business to ensure a good level of representation and ownership. Because co-creation is essential, we encourage holding interactive workshops with colleagues to get to the information required. Transparency is crucial in any Customer Experience Transformation. Hence the outputs should be available to all your employees and they need to be written and communicated in a language that everyone can understand. So, no technical or business jargon!

Sometimes it is necessary to translate a document to meet the needs of the target audience. For instance, although you may have an overall Customer Experience Strategy document, when presenting to the Sales department, you may adapt what you offer to ensure it engages them. However, the overall objectives and target experience should be aligned across all departments.

Within CX CENTRIC there are nine core outputs that we recommend. These nine key documents combine to answer four key questions:

- What is the experience we currently offer to our customers?

- What is the target experience that we want to offer to our customers?

- What is the gap between the experience we currently offer and our target experience?

- What is our plan of action to bridge the gap between the current and target experience?

CX Strategy

Once you have decided that you will prioritise the experience of your customers, you will need to define your Customer Experience Strategy (CX Strategy). The CX Strategy outlines the target experience you intend to offer to your customers. In essence, you are defining how you want your customers to feel while interacting with your business. And you may also want to identify key descriptive words such as 'easy', 'impressive' or 'fast'. We refer to these as: 'experience principles'. The CX Strategy also defines the linkage of the customer experience strategy to your organisation's overall objectives. And shows how it is aligned to your organisation's brand values.

The intention of the CX Strategy is to create a shared internal goal, which relates to your customers. And to align business goals with a customer-focused culture. The idea is to produce a document that is very simple and very clear so it can be communicated and shared across the organisation. The CX Strategy also is a basis to enable the development of specific employee behaviours that reflect your brand values and the organisation's mission.

Without a CX Strategy, your organisation may still be able to improve the customer's experience, just by focusing on the basics. But having a CX Strategy allows a company to be very efficient and focused. It also is a key enabler to be able to offer a differentiated experience, which organisations use to gain a competitive advantage in the marketplace.

CASE STUDY

Translating the Customer Strategy

Rajeev Karkhanis

Chief Consultant at XperienceByDesign, India

When tasked with implementing a customer experience transformation for a large national organisation in India, we began by producing the CX Strategy. Once the CX Strategy was produced I realised it would need to be translated for each department. We then conducted workshops with colleagues across the organisation to turn this into an actionable statement unique to their department. Asking the critical question: 'What does this strategy mean for me?'

As with all artefacts in the CXCENTRIC playbook, the CX Strategy should not be written in isolation. Here are a few tips to help you along the way:

- Engage senior management to participate in the creation of the CX Strategy

- Ensure there is alignment between your CX Strategy and overall Corporate Objectives

- We recommend that you update your CX Strategy once per year at the very least

- Ensure that your CX Strategy is physically printed and placed somewhere where all employees can see it

- Develop experience principles and be very specific about the employee behaviours that you want to see

CX Register

At the beginning of your Customer Experience transformation, there will be many employees who already have great ideas about how to improve the Customer Experience. As your transformation continues on its journey employees who are interested and engaged will always offer their suggestions. At a minimum in any programme, we advise you to have a central location which is accessible by employees, where they can add their insights, recommendations and feedback based on their experience. This is the purpose of the CX Register.

If your employees are supportive of the change, you are likely to receive a lot more items listed in the CX Register than is possible to implement. Hence the next challenge is to begin to add some attributes to the items in the CX Register so that you can triage and prioritise effectively. At a minimum, you should identify the stage in the customer journey that the result will impact, the impacted customer segment and also the level of impact (high, medium or low). Also, you may choose to add other attributes such as the teams that will be impacted, the number of days required from a specific team, technologies impacted and general difficulty. This information will make it more comfortable as you discuss and make decisions in the CX Prioritisation session.

Many organisations use software to store these suggestions. This ensures that the information is always accessible and also makes it easier to change and update information as you analyse further.

REMEMBER

Remember, there is no such thing as a 'silly' suggestion. The CX Register is a great way to get employees across the organisation engaged and to encourage them to start thinking about improving the CX.

As well as suggestions about general improvements to the Customer Experience, the CX Register should also contain industry best practices that you may want to trial and even new processes and tools. Hence we encourage you to keep up to date about what is happening in the market. This puts you in a position to pick and choose tools and best practices which can simplify and streamline the way you manage Customer Experience and the insights that you can generate.

CX Shortlist

During the CX Prioritisation session, the team discusses customer insights and recommendations listed in the CX Register. One of the outputs of this event must be your agreed CX Shortlist. The CX Shortlist defines the experience deliverables that your organisation commits to delivering during a given cadence. We recommend a cadence of 3 months. Once created, the team should avoid adding other items to the shortlist and should aim to deliver everything on the list.

The CX Shortlist should be aligned to your CX Strategy and hence have a positive impact on your organisations overall corporate objectives. Some organisations may choose to split the Shortlist between Customer Experience and Employee Experience, depending on how large and complex the list becomes. It is also an idea to split the shortlist between by CX Pillar as per the CXPA, or even just size. The idea is to agree on a list that is as simple as possible and that can be communicated across an organisation and be well understood.

It is essential to have a clear story to justify the items on the list, to ensure that you take your employees on the journey with you. You are likely to be asked why other things were not shortlisted. Take this sort of interest as positive; it shows that your employees care about the experience they give to the customers. Ensure that you respond as openly and honestly as possible. To make your life easier, it is best practice to refer to customer insights to justify why certain items have been prioritised.

The CX Manager coordinates and drives employees across the organisation to deliver the CX Shortlist. However, the CX Manager must do so with the support of their team and the Directors. Please note that although the CX Manager is coordinating, the CX Shortlist will identify the senior executives who are responsible for the resolution and implementation of actions on the Shortlist.

Journey Mapping and Customer Personas

Creation of customer journey maps is an essential part of the CX CENTRIC playbook. A customer journey map is a visual representation of the path people take when interacting with organisations, services, products and brands.

Journey mapping helps ensure that employees across the entire organisation have a shared view of the customer journey. When driving an organisation toward customer-centricity, it is essential to initiate the journey mapping process and ensure that your team is able to map out accurately and depict various customer touchpoints and identify interdependencies across people, processes and technology that impact the overall CX.

There are often different layers to a journey mapping process which are usually differentiated by the level of detail and information fed into the map at each particular stage. It is best to start building a very high-level journey map first and then drill into further detail where necessary. Please note that the journey does not begin when your customer signs up for your product or service. It starts much earlier than that.

While journey mapping, an organisation must look at the journey from a customer's perspective and keep in mind that interactions with a business represent only a fraction of an overall customer journey. Which is where customer personas prove to be useful as they are crafted in the first-person narrative format, which helps organisations identify with customers' needs and challenges.

Enhanced with research data from customer interviews, a combination of journey maps and personas will help build empathy with customers, build brand loyalty and improve product or service. Customer personas are part and parcel of the journey mapping process. A customer persona is a fictional character that represents various types of customers who might be using your service, product, site, or brand in a similar way. By learning about your customers' traits, values, experiences, aspirations and pain points, you can dramatically improve customer experience, strengthen brand loyalty and boost sales. More often than not, businesses create multiple personas for their journey maps to correctly map out the customer journey of each persona type.

Not every customer is the same. Too many organisations make generalisations about their customers and end up merging the needs of different types of customers together. The result is a product offering which never really hits the mark with any specific customer group. As the saying goes: If you try to please everyone you end up pleasing no-one. We use customer personas to formalise the analysis of different customer groups.

The below is an example of a Customer Persona created using UXPressia, a tool for creating Customer Journey Maps as well as Customer Personas.

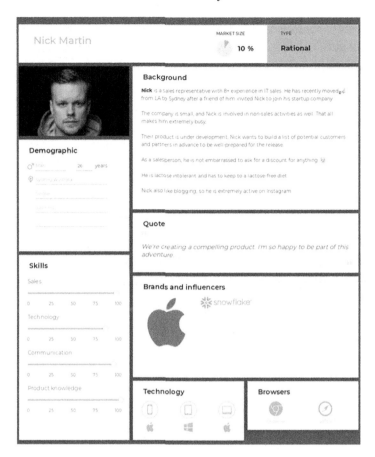

Aside from better outlining an overall customer experience, a journey map also allows you to conduct gap analysis against, which compares the experience that you currently offer to the targeted experience outlined in your Experience Strategy. Armed with a journey map, you can also identify pain points which are considered as sub-optimal customer experiences. Immediately this will put you in a strong position to be able to recommend actionable items which you can add to your Experience Register. These can then be discussed during the CX Prioritisation meeting. After completing your customer journey map, it should be clear where the gaps are, at which stage of the journey they occur and which customer persona is affected by them.

As you mature in your journey towards customer-centricity and continue to apply the CX CENTRIC model, you will also begin to identify key moments of truth of your customers. Moments of truth are the moments when a customer/user interacts with a brand, product or service to form or change an impression about your brand, product or service. These should also be indicated on the customer journey map and are often used to distinguish or reinforce your brand promise.

It is best to begin mapping out your first customer journey by using a whiteboard and post-it stickers. Later on, digitize your map by transferring your physical journey map to a journey mapping software.

Here's what Yuri Vedenin, the founder of UXPressia, has to say about the use of customer journey mapping software to drive CX improvement:

 **CASE STUDY** The Power of Journey Mapping

Yuri Vedenin

Director of Uxpressia

Our online journey mapping platform became a hub of CX projects for companies large and small across the globe. Some of our clients create paper-based journey maps during workshops and then digitize them in UXPressia in order to share and collaborate with their teammates and also present the maps online. We find that companies working with distributed teams end up creating maps online from the start. We also find that many teams end up making journey mapping templates with UXPressia which they then print out and use in real-life workshops.

Another great example is a consulting client of ours. It's a 1000-employee legal tech company that makes a suite of legal directories and provides data analytics services. We helped them implement a journey mapping framework which they now use to drive CX transformation during workshops and beyond. Their goal is to make sure that every business process is 100% tested through the CJM framework built with the help of UXPressia tools.

You may wonder: why do you need to keep a digital copy of your journey map? Because your journey map isn't a do-it-once-and-forget-about-it kind of document. Neither is it a pretty visual piece to impress a client or an executive in your company.

For customer journey mapping to become a change agent in an organisation, it's essential to treat your journey map as a living and breathing document that must be accessible to your team and updated regularly. Customer journey mapping should always be a collaborative effort between the team and the many stakeholders. I encourage you to involve them all in this process by organizing a customer journey mapping workshop.

 **TOP TIP**

Getting the most out of Journey Mapping

Yuri Vedenin

Director of Uxpressia

When it comes to inviting teammates to your customer journey mapping workshop, there are a few rules that you need to follow.

Invite those team members who can share knowledge about actual customer journeys. These can be:

• *Customer service and sales reps. They are the ones who talk with your customers face-to-face. There are lots of ideas and insights they can share so they are your VIP guests.*

• *Marketing folks, customer experience specialists and researchers (including the ones who do usability tests, web analytics reviews, etc.). Even if they don't talk to the customers, they know a lot about how things are going with your customer journey here and now.*

• *Product owners if they communicate with customers and have a more or less clear idea of what the customer journey looks like at the moment.*

Even though these people might not take part in the transformation process and implement the changes on their own, you need their input to fill in the gaps in the customer journey and enable them to share knowledge they have.

We also encourage you to invite those people to workshops who will bring your journey maps to life and

110

implement the changes. They can have little to no knowledge about the as-is customer journey, but it's these people whose work will be directly affected by whatever you might discover during the workshop. In this case, their roles can be pretty much the same as above. Plus, think about inviting the IT folks, office managers and any other internal roles who will take part in the journey mapping implementation process.

Invite the organisation's influencers and decision makers. As long as you want to get time and resources for further customer experience improvement, you need them aboard.

Besides, these folks do not often communicate with customers directly and therefore might have a very vague idea what experiences their customers are going through and what pain points they face. Showing them the areas of opportunity is bound to be an eye-opener and the first step to an improved customer experience process within the organisation.

Needless to say, there is more than one way to conduct a customer journey mapping workshop. We shared the approach we use at UXPressia and hope it gives you a good head start."

Jonathan Daniels

Roles and Responsibilities Matrix

The roles and responsibilities matrix presents the job tasks outlined in the 'Teams' section of the framework and associates them with named individuals. This should be completed and agreed as a collective exercise.

Within the 'Teams' section of the CX CENTRIC framework, we outline the roles required along with the tasks, attributes and knowledge required. In practice, you may or may not have individuals with these specific job titles. On the contrary, as part of your Customer Experience transformation, you are likely to bring in people or take people out where necessary. This usually is dependent on what needs to be delivered and depending on their general workload. Hence it is imperative that your team regularly review the core actions that are required, understand if they are being executed or not, and pinpoint who is performing them. You can then ensure that any missed actions are assigned. And you can also verify that everyone agrees with their actions.

Roles and responsibilities should be reviewed every quarter. The first workshop where you produce the matrix is always the most time-consuming; after this, it becomes more of a confirmation exercise with a few tweaks and some discussion. The overall objective is to ensure clear accountability on your transformation, which improves efficiency and keeps confusion to a minimal.

ACTIVITY

Have a discussion with your team about their roles and responsibilities. Have they remained constant over time, or have there been changes? Are there any responsibilities that they do not feel comfortable with? Are there any responsibilities where they need more support? This sort of information can help improve your chance of delivering improvements quickly and accurately if managed correctly.

Change Assessment and Planning

As mentioned previously, one of the core pillars of the CX CENTRIC framework is Change Management. As a CX leader, you must always remember that you are primarily running a business change activity. And managing change is a specialist skill, requiring tenacity.

A crucial part of the CX CENTRIC framework is to review the CX Shortlist and to carry out a business impact assessment. This is where we consider the items contained in the CX Shortlist and determine which teams will be affected, the level of impact and give some specific details. Once this is complete, you will be in a position to begin the creation of your change plan.

The change plan highlights the actions required to ensure that specific people in each department are adequately supported. This usually requires activities such as training, communications, testing, process changes, organizational structure, or data changes. Hence these need to be planned, tracked and monitored.

We recommend bringing in members from across the organization who have a good level of knowledge of the different teams. Hence a vital part of the CX Leader role is creating healthy relationships across the business. This then makes it easier to identify the impacts and agree the change plan.

 Promoting cross-functional discussion

Tonja Pena

Principle Consultant @ Capital eXperience Group

I always encourage a cross-functional conversation with other department leads that will be affected by the change. This is to understand how the initiatives will impact processes and policies, and evaluate what type of technology will be needed, re-configured as well as what skill set will be needed by employees at any level so that those affected departments can plan for and prioritize the changes accordingly.

ACTIVITY

Pick a department and work with them to make a list of all the initiatives which are planned for the next 6 months. How much change is coming? How will your CX related changes be incorporated? Will they be overburdened?

Experience Horizon

The experience Horizon is an output of the CX Prioritisation session. It gives a high-level plan of the customer experience deliverables over the next 6 to 12 months. Although you may have produced a CX Strategy as a Customer Experience Leader, without a clear route to achieve this strategy, how can you be sure that the strategy will be achieved? To believe in the CX Strategy your employees will need the Experience Horizon, which will help them to see what the future experience will look like and the path we will take. When employees are clear on what they can expect over the long term, it often reduces the fear of loss of job.

The Experience Horizon often sets apart the good from the great. It supports alignment within an organization and helps an organization to remain and become more efficient. By outlining the Experience Horizon, it makes it a lot easier when prioritizing and selecting items for the CX Shortlist.

Depending on the audience and the purpose of the conversation, we recommend that the Experience Horizon is split in different ways. For instance, it is often divided by department. By outlining the changes coming, which affect various departments, we can then target our communications better. It is also divided by level of complexity, or even by the CXPA pillars. We recommend breaking down your experience Horizon up in different ways; this gives you the ammunition available for whenever you need to use it.

ACTIVITY

List the key projects that your organisation has committed to working on over the next 6 months.

1. Identify the teams which will be involved for each project.

2. Use the labels: High, Medium and Low, to estimate the amount of work involved for each team.

3. Are there particular teams which appear to have too much work? Consider speaking to the team in order to present this issue and find solutions together.

Engagement Plan

As a leader of a Customer Experience Transformation, you must bring your employees with you on the journey. Hence the communications and activities proposed must be thought through and planned in detail. This is done through an engagement plan. The engagement plan drives employee engagement and involvement and is targeted at all employees from front line staff to the executive suite. The engagement plan will also explain how you will communicate the shared understanding of the CX Strategy, along with the Experience Roadmap.

The Engagement plan outlines the different groups of employees. It presents the content, timeframe and format, along with the underlying objective. Please note that this is different from a communication plan. Influential leaders give lots of opportunity to employees for co-creation and ensure that communication is always a two-way street. The engagement plan must offer lots of opportunity to reinforce the customer-centric mindset, often through reward and recognition strategies. This must be clearly defined to avoid ambiguity.

There is a lot of exciting and motivating content which you can use as part of your engagement plan. Such as:

- Reward and recognition strategies

- Regularly review CX metrics and feedback at all levels of the organisation

- Opportunities for co-creation with employees

- Collect and share stories of CX excellence at your company

- Communication strategies and tactics to share the importance of CX with employees, customers and the company

- Communicate and engage employees at all levels of the organisation in the elements of the CX strategy

- Strategies to communicate metrics and ROI with employee and stakeholder groups

- Develop and deliver ongoing CX interaction training to employees

To make your engagement plan effective, the way that you communicate is very important. Different people are receptive to different and varied forms of communication, so apply a mix of different methods to ensure that you connect with your employees. Also, take time to make your conversations exciting. Avoid presenting things that are uninteresting or irrelevant to your target audience. Use the marketing department to help with this, as they would already have good experience in this domain. Consider hiring a graphic designer to help with the look and feel of your messages. Considering that connecting with your employees is a critical success to your programme you can justify the investment.

Once you've created your plan and produced the content, your task doesn't stop there. Take time to collect feedback regarding how your employees felt after the activity or message is complete. Do they feel more motivated? Are they clear on the target experience that you want to give your customers? What separates our customer experience from that of our competitors?

Remember that the aim is to engage "hearts and minds" of the organisation across employee groups, hence this is what needs to be measured as far as possible.

Business Case

The Business Case is a justification for the investment in your programme on the basis of expected commercial outcomes and benefits. The business case should also detail how these outcomes and benefits will be tracked, in order to measure the return on investment.

This is often the part that is the most difficult for CX specialists. It's not because we don't think that what we do offers benefit, it's just that often there are so many factors affecting the result that it is difficult to attribute a change in a KPI to one particular action. But this doesn't mean that it is something that you should miss out. It's the same in the world of finance; a portfolio manager has the task of managing a portfolio of investments, they conduct research and analyse potential investment opportunities then make the best decisions they can, based on the information available. After a year when you review how your investments are doing, there are often several external factors and factors which you could never have imagined which have a significant impact on the share price. Hence Wealth Managers get through this by having a solid strategy and good tactics. This is the same for CX.

The business case should communicate the importance of the customer experience strategy to deliver the organisation's business goals. And it should present a clear correlation between improved experiences and business outcomes such as growth, attrition and profitability. If this link is not present, you will have a tough time convincing others to invest.

Within your business case, you should also identify how you will measure your success. Be specific about the key metrics that you will use. And be clear about how you will be able to produce these metrics. This is something that often companies are not used to doing. However, this is a critical success factor for your CX transformation so put the effort in! We dive into a lot more detail on the development of metrics when we discuss the ICON process.

"Metrics should be designed for People. People should not be designed for Metrics"

Ali Malik CCXP, Head of CX Projects, Static A

The CX Playbook

This above quote rings so true in the world of B2B subscription models where customer success teams are increasingly combining CX with tangible measured business results. For customer success to prove its worth to their own companies, it first needs to prove its worth to their customers.

Different approaches are put into place to help customers measure added value and ROI. Sue Nabeth Moore, customer success leader (founder of Success Track Enterprise and co-founder of Customer Success Mastermind) has coined the A.M.P.M. (Adoption Measurement and Performance Measurement) methodology.

TOP TIP

Defining adoption and performance indicators with AMPM

Sue Nabeth Moore

Customer Success Leader

The A.M.P.M. approach can be applied to any product or service and implies defining adoption and performance indicators. The adoption indicators are considered as the pre-requisite measurements to control that the path for the desired outcome necessary for success is paved. This often implies the adoption and measurement of new routines, reflexes and adaptations to organisation and processes. It's no longer a question of doing business as usual but moving out of a known comfort zone. Performance indicators measure the improvement in expected business results as they are achieved. Depending on the context, solution/service type and expected business outcomes, the A.M.P.M. indicators are adapted. The ROI of products and services can then be more easily measured thanks to the analysis of the performance measurements. The example below applies to a CRM application:

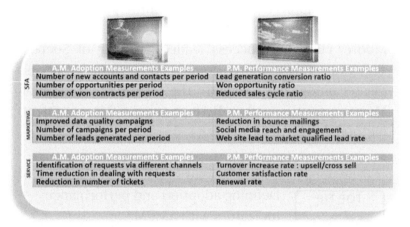

	A.M. Adoption Measurements Examples	P.M. Performance Measurements Examples
SFA	Number of new accounts and contacts per period Number of opportunities per period Number of won contracts per period	Lead generation conversion ratio Won opportunity ratio Reduced sales cycle ratio
MARKETING	Improved data quality campaigns Number of campaigns per period Number of leads generated per period	Reduction in bounce mailings Social media reach and engagement Web site lead to market qualified lead rate
SERVICE	Identification of requests via different channels Time reduction in dealing with requests Reduction in number of tickets	Turnover increase rate : upsell/cross sell Customer satisfaction rate Renewal rate

Source: Sue Nabeth Moore – Success Track Enterprise

Customer Success (CS) and Customer Experience share the common ground of customer loyalty and delivering pristine experiences and pertinent engagement across customer journeys. Together both CX and CS create a win-win business situation: CX locks consumer/customer engagement and CS locks business outcomes and ROI.

The CX CENTRIC™ playbook offers a sturdy platform to plan how you will successfully govern your Customer Experience activities. However, like most things, it must be adapted to align with the make-up of your organisation. Yes, there may be some changes that your organisation can make to adapt to the framework but if the difference is too heavy for most of the participants, they are very likely to reject it. Therefore as you apply this framework be very mindful of its impact on the day-to-day activities of the participants. Also, deviating from the structure is never a problem, but the impact must be managed. For example, maybe you decide to reduce the frequency of some of the meetings? So you decide that you will hold the organisation-wide communication meeting less frequently. Moving away from the proposed frequency is not a problem but the impact on other events and tasks should be analysed to make sure that the governance still works overall for you. For this, we suggest the support of a Customer Experience Coach to help guide and ease you through the implementation process.

The ICON process offers a clear path to manage your Customer-Centric Transformation. In this section, I present each of the four steps of the process. I aim to give you the relevant information you need and try to keep it as simple as possible.

Jonathan Daniels

INITIATE

INITIATE

 CX AUDIT

 IDENTIFY QUICK WINS

 HIGH LEVEL JOURNEY MAPS

 CHALLENGE KPIS

 AGREE TRANSFORMATION OBJECTIVES

 BUILD RELATIONSHIPS

The initiation phase offers a practitioner the chance to set the transformation up for success. This often begins with an audit of the customer experience capabilities, as well as an analysis of the current Customer Knowledge available and the established processes to create that knowledge. A key goal at this stage is to identify as many quick wins as possible; these are low effort high impact items which can bring a positive ROI for your programme. We suggest you begin with reducing customer friction, as research shows that this has the highest impact on customer loyalty. During this phase, you begin to build key relationships, constructing a team with representatives from all areas of the business. In addition, you take bold but calculated steps to set the tone for the rest of the transformation.

There is sometimes a lot of noise in organisations concerning documents. "It's not in the right format", or "I didn't sign off on this!", or the worst: "Why wasn't I informed?" In the early stages of the initiation phase, set the tone correctly. Here are a few rules which you can consider publishing:

- All CX docs are available in read-only format for anyone who wants to see them

- These documents are working documents, so don't judge us on the presentation at this stage, but please feel free to feedback about the content

- If you have a suggestion feel free to add it to the CX Register

At this early stage, you can introduce the Experience

Register and Experience Shortlist and begin to firm up the contents of these documents. Remember these are living documents and their contents should be readily available for anyone to see.

Pace is very important. Different organisations work at different paces. Try to speak to different employees about current and previous projects to get a gauge of how fast they work and run your plans by as many people as possible. Taking on too much work can detail the most meticulous of plans.

Customer Experience Audit

Starting out with the ICON process is always exciting. If you are a consultant, often you are meeting new people and if you are a leader within your organisation, you are setting sail towards new territory. Carrying out an audit of your current Customer Experience capabilities gives your programme a strong foundation. We cannot enter an organisation and immediately begin to administer solutions. How would you feel if when you visit your medical doctor, they administer medicine to you without asking you what symptoms you have? We must begin by gathering as much information as possible, holding back our assumptions, avoiding to make sweeping statements.

If we refer back to the Customer Experience Alignment model mentioned in the early chapters, at this stage, we are focusing on Customer Experience Strategy as well as the CX infrastructure and processes. However, do not neglect the importance of reviewing the level of functional integration. There are many organisations that offer Customer Experience audits and health checks. Once you have completed your health check, you will then be in a better place to decide where to focus your attention.

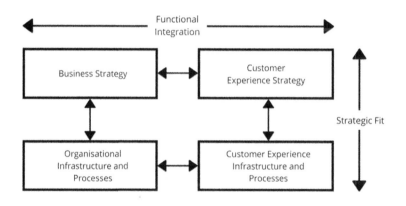

Identify Quick wins

Whenever anyone invests in anything new, there is always some form of doubt and worry. We often give a new investment a window of opportunity, often a fixed period of time, to prove itself. For instance, I am not a gambler, simply because I have very low patience when it comes to losing money. I remember the first time I tried scratch cards. I bought three scratch cards and didn't win anything substantial. So after that, in my head, I made a decision that scratch cards are a waste of money. Many people will have the same approach to your CX transformation programme. They will often mentally decide on the number of months that they will give you the 'benefit of the doubt' and if you haven't provided real value in this timeframe, then it's very likely thay will begin to question the credibility of the programme.

To overcome this, your programme must identify quick wins early on to prove that it is worth the investment. As CX professionals, we know the power and profitability of investing in CX, and we can talk about it all day. But keep the talking to a minimum at this stage. Even if you manage to trap someone in the corridor and they appeared to be interested as you bounced a few ideas off them. This activity is about providing proof so that people in your organisation can experience the benefit first hand. This is about honing in on a few key improvements you can make, often described as 'low hanging fruit'. A friend of mine used to always tell me, work hard but work smart at the same time. These low hanging fruits are the smart option for you at this stage. These will have a high impact on Customer Experience and are reasonably easy to implement. To guide your choice on what to focus on consider plotting the items from your CX Register into the following matrix.

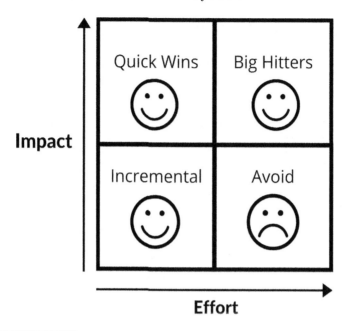

Impact

Effort

TOP TIP

Accurately identifying the quick wins

Tonja Pena

Principle Consultant @ Capital eXperience Group

I recommend starting with problems that have been captured by the customer repeatedly, or that stand out as challenges or gaps in the customer journey. This will ensure that the priorities are objectively agreed on by the organisation, customers and front-line employees collectively. Trying to quantify the impact those problems have in terms of CSat or NPS scores can help prioritise where to start and you can, at least internally, also understand the impact these challenges have on revenue in repeat business or referrals. You'll want to prioritise the problems that have the most impact and will take the least effort to implement.

High Level Journey Maps

In the opening stages, we recommend producing very high-level Customer Journey maps. The idea is that you begin to guide the team to understand the journey of the customer and to start to think about things from the customer's perspective. At this stage, we only need to go in enough detail to begin to uncover the key pain points, positive points, moments of truth and the overall journey.

Remind people that this is the opening phase and avoid going into too much detail. You want to keep things as simple as possible to keep the customer experience conversation accessible to anyone who wants to join. Don't think that you impress people by plotting thousands of touchpoints on your customer journey. A simple picture of the customer journey, which is clear and concise is sufficient at this point. At this stage, you are trying to attract people to build your network, so that going forward they can support your programme.

For many people, it may be the first time that they have come across or spent time focusing on Customer Experience. Many of them may never have given a thought as to how their job actually relates to the end customer. These journey maps will lead employees to re-question their role and to think about where they fit in the overall puzzle.

Identifying, Listening and Challenging KPIs

As mentioned in the opening chapters, strong leaders are results-driven. Hence analysis and evaluation of current KPIs is always a powerful place to start. Now this should generally be covered in any good customer experience audit. However, I have expanded on this point as it is a critical success factor for any CX transformation.

At this stage in the programme, a CX Leader should spend time sitting and working with each department to pinpoint how they measure success. Remember that each department normally has their own set of things to focus on. For instance, the sales department will often have quarterly sales targets, broken down by market segment. The technology department will often measure success by the number of projects delivered on time and within budget. The marketing department measures success by evaluating the return on investment for each of their marketing channels. Every department has their own definition of what good looks like for them. You will then be in a better position to be able to relate to them and you will be able to aim for shared outcomes which will motivate them to support your programme. In addition to this, you can also begin to challenge the KPIs. How do these align to what the customers experience? Is there even a link? If so, how strong is this relationship? These sorts of questions encourage teams to begin to think about their work differently. Now they can begin to consider the impact they have on the lives of your customers.

CASE STUDY

"What gets measured, gets managed"

Naeem Arif

Director of United Carpets, UK

At United Carpets we used to focus on NPS and this was great to measure how well we were generally going. However, we worked out that this was more of a reflection. In reality, what we wanted to know is: 'What percentage of our customers become repeat customers?' We decided to move from NPS to RPR (repeat purchase rate) and started measuring both NPS and RPR. Now we have started measuring this, we aim to get our RPR at more than 60% and this is something we review on a quarterly basis.

Agree transformation objectives

At this early stage, a leader must set the direction for the teams involved. This direction must be presented clearly, so that there is little chance of misinterpretation. Customer experience is a very broad subject. And hence you will not have a shortage of choice here. But your objectives should align to the objectives of the business as a whole. These objectives need to be very clear, as this is what your programme will be measured against.

For many of you starting off in organisations which are new to CX, your objectives should include the setup of a Customer Experience Strategy. Although at this stage, the Customer Experience Strategy may not be very detailed, it gives your team something to measure the customer journey against. Remember, Rome wasn't built in a day. You should start at a simple point when defining your Customer Experience Strategy. And as the insights of your programme continue to develop, you can begin to flesh out and improve your CX Strategy positioning your organisation to benefit from any opportunities uncovered.

At this stage, you won't know everything, but there are a lot of stakeholders who may have their own ideas of what good objectives may look like. Be upfront and ask them about their ideas when you speak to them. Give yourselves the opportunity to agree to the objectives collectively. The objectives should link to positive outcomes for the customer and for the organisation.

Build Relationships

I spoke about building relationships in the opening chapters. Invest in the right people and they will pay you back in dividends throughout your programme. And this is true in any walk of life. At this stage spend time getting to know people. What are their hopes and dreams? What would they like to achieve over the next year? What are they interested in? What are their key challenges? By connecting with people on a personal level, you are then able to understand how you can help them throughout your transformation. After all, the transformation is about them.

By investing in relationships early on, you put

yourself in a position of power. Ever heard of: "Your network is your net worth"? This principle will apply in your transformation too. As you learn more about the individuals in different teams, you will then build an idea about which people you can assign to certain tasks. After all, often you will require support from a cross-functional team who will still have to carry out their normal work. Hence you rely on strong relationships in the initial stages to help build momentum.

TOP TIP Seek and learn from the best

Janelle Mansfield

Amplified CX

As you build this plan, consider who in your organization has the best track record of successful implementations. Leverage them and their knowledge to build a comprehensive plan that covers both the operational (process & technology) side, as well as the people side.

REMEMBER

Investing in relationships is not a one-time activity. A relationship is just like a plant. We must continue to nourish our relationships to see them grow. And failing to nourish them will cause them to wither away. Plan time in your day to invest in relationships with key personnel across your organisation.

Jonathan Daniels

CO-CREATE

CO-CREATE

DELIVER QUICK WINS

DELIVER FOUNDATION TRAINING

MORE DETAILED JOURNEY MAPS

TRAINING NEEDS ASSESSMENT

ESTABLISH CUSTOMER CENTRIC KPIS

As you transition from the initiation phase, you begin to operate with the cross-functional team that you have assembled. You work closely with your team to evaluate and deliver some quick wins. This not only demonstrates your ability to affect change, but it also helps to build momentum for your team.

By this point you should be able to firm up some customer-centric KPIs which link to the KPIs that departments are already working with. You may introduce journey maps and go into more detail at certain points where necessary. You may hold your first CX Prioritisation event, which will lead to the update of your Experience Shortlist and the creation of your Experience Horizon. It is also likely that you will have produced a draft version of your Experience Strategy. You may also firm up a basic training needs analysis to help along the way. A key objective at this stage is to set an atmosphere of transparency, encouragement and positivity. Your team members need to be free to make mistakes, to take risks and to be creative while improving the customer experience.

After a long winter of hibernation, ants normally come out of their nests and begin scurrying around becoming re-accustomed to their surroundings. At this time the queen ants spend time laying eggs underground. In order to keep the eggs warm, worker ants warm themselves up from the sun's rays, then quickly head back to the nest to transfer some of that heat to the next generation of ants to come. This atmosphere of selfless collaboration is what needs to be promoted in order to drive a true level of customer centricity on your programme.

CASE STUDY

Tales from a Fortune 100 CX Transformation

Ruth Crowley

Fortune 100 Retail Company

One notable success was in a Fortune 100 Retail Company. Prior projects failed without purposeful engagement of associates across the organisation. The CX Design Group was very conscientious about research, analysis, design, prototyping and Journey Mapping. The "formal" initiation was then activated engaging key stakeholders, so they were informed. In some cases, they also had to be "convinced". Shifting paradigms is not for the weak of heart! What we learned was when people understood the process they became actively engaged. If they were included it helped ensure ownership across functions. The organisational silos had to be flattened – or horizontalised! Reviewing Journey Maps stimulated a new awareness and shared understanding of how the process worked and where the gaps were, in the internal delivery system and in delivery to the end consumer. We leveraged Journey Maps to introduce co-creation promoting ownership prior to operationalisation. Prototypes were first used in the field to allow a fact-based test prior to investing in models. Customer and Associate feedback was included. Applying early learning and adapting the model reduced the financial investment and informed the best go-forward model. As the solution rolled out the active inclusion and nurturing of Associates continued. Successes were widely shared and celebrated.

Momentum grew and the results in the first month showed an increase of 35%. Not all believed initially, but sustainable results directed the expansion of the project which continues today.

TOP TIP

The focus of a CX transformation should not be on the CX leader. The focus of the CX transformation is about the result and impact for the customer and about the change felt by the employees. This leads to more growth. Mobilise the team and co-create as much as possible.

Deliver quick wins

During the initiation phase, there were a number of 'quick wins' which you identified. Now it's time for you to work with your team to ensure they are delivered. This helps build credibility for your team, as it proves that you are able to drive tangible results. Keep in mind that the objective of this phase is not just to deliver, but to co-deliver. This is the opportunity to build bridges across organisational silos. This is your chance to give opportunities to others who want to advance their career. This is not about you; this is about you building a cross-departmental team and giving them the autonomy to deliver improvements to the experience.

These quick wins help to increase cohesion between teams. Also, when these results are communicated across the organisation it encourages others to want to get involved.

TOP TIP

Didn't deliver all the quick wins? This is not a huge issue. The team may still be new to working in this way. Some teams take longer than others to find their rhythm. Put the issue of late delivery on the agenda of your retrospective meeting and ask the team to brainstorm together to agree on some solutions.

Deliver foundation of training

At this stage, you should be well underway to building strong relationships across your organisation. In addition, you will have already conducted a customer experience audit, so you will have a high-level understanding of the strengths, weaknesses, opportunities and threats for your team to grow. So now is the time to deliver a foundation of customer experience training. Everyone across the organisation should have the same understanding of what you refer to as "customer experience". Create clarity around definitions of key terminology to avoid confusion.

Take care to tailor your training to specific target groups. Use the knowledge you gained about the important KPIs of each department to taylor language and examples which will resonate with your audience. Ensure that leaders, team members and the wider organisation have a good level of knowledge about the concepts and benefits of CX and also understand broadly what you are planning to achieve.

Training is about sharing knowledge with your colleagues. The customer experience audit will identify the gaps in knowledge and tackling these gaps should be your objective in the initial training which you give. It is equally about showing employees what they are missing out on and stirring their passion to get involved with the programme. Be creative when you design your training. Remember it's great to show them what customer experience is and how you plan to deliver. But also, it's important for them to feel and understand your passion. The positive energy that you give is an investment for your programme. When your participants feel how excited you are about becoming customer-centric, many will make a decision at that point to want to learn more and to support your endeavours.

More detailed Journey Maps

At this stage, now is the time to dive a bit deeper into customer journey maps. Where are the opportunities for improvement? Where are the pain points? Where are the points which could be used to differentiate your offering? Ask yourself key questions and continue to build knowledge about your customers. Ensure that you keep a balanced approach to customer journey mapping. Obtain input from employees across a wide range of departments. Combine this with data and customers too. And also, only dive as detailed as you need to. If you are producing information which is not actionable, re-consider to verify if this truly is time well spent. CX Leaders often fail by not monitoring the usefulness and effectiveness of journey mapping activities.

REMEMBER

Remember less is always more and besides, if you create 300 journey maps who will read them?

Training Needs Assessment

In this phase, although you will be delivering a foundational level of training, please note that your training plan should not end there! In the co-creation phase, the team is practicing and forming customer-centric habits. They are also making mistakes and reflecting on these during retrospective sessions. And they are discovering new territory. This may be the first time that certain team members carry out some of the activities that you are introducing. It may be the first time that some team members hold certain responsibilities. Hence it is important to review the capabilities of the team along with the challenges that they are facing, to establish more targeted needs for training.

Establish Customer-Centric KPIs and Metrics

At this stage, you will be in a position to establish customer-centric KPIs. These are KPIs which the customers care about and hence have an impact on the customer experience. This is critical for the long-term success of the organisation, as well as the success of your programme. Years ago, I worked with a large organisation in Europe. The directors spent two days conducting a prioritisation exercise to agree on the projects that would be undertaken over the next six months. Only 2 out of 40 projects would have a positive impact on the customer's experience.

Often in large organisations, departments tend to become self-justifying and self-reinforcing. The link between their activity and customer value erodes. Establishing customer-centric KPIs helps organisations understand how customer-centric they really are. This reality can be a wake-up call for many people. This harsh reality can be very effective to help build momentum by creating a sense of urgency to re-focus on the customer.

KPIs are often very high level and they help to identify overall trends. However, at this stage, it is important to get into the details. The Case Study below is a great example of how to develop actionable CX metrics.

 **Building Customer-Centric metrics**

Kerri Nelson

CEO of Customer First Now

Once we know which customer touchpoints are painful and critical to your customers, we conduct an analysis of the CX data inputs. Some of these include:

• *Journey Maps – identify touchpoints that are both Moments of Truth and Pain Points*

• *Customer Service and Complaint reason codes – identify top reasons for customers contacting for help and top reasons for complaints*

• *Survey "write-in" comments – understand top opportunity area themes*

• *Customer-facing KPI's – review internal operational metrics to see which are not achieving best practice levels, e.g. On-Time Delivery %; Speed of Answer (in seconds); Time to Search (in seconds)*

We then determine the criteria by which to prioritise existing and new metrics. An example of our comparison chart is presented below. This is normally conducted in a Scorecard Workshop, where we aim to determine the top 10 metrics. This workshop is conducted with key operational staff as well as CX leaders.

Example Metric	Customer Facing?	Moment of Truth or Customer Pain Point?	Linkage to CX Strategy?
Average speed of answer (for telephone)	Yes	No	Yes - demonstrates sense of urgency
On time delivery	Yes	Yes	Yes
Retention	No	No	Yes
First Contact Resolution	Yes	Yes	Yes
Data Accuracy	Yes	Yes	Yes
Average Handle Time	No	No	No

Once the prioritised list has been established, we research 'best practices' in order to be sure that the goals will resonate *with customers. We then assign owners to each metric. The following table is an example of a CX Scorecard:*

Customer Delight Metric Driver		Owner	Goal	April 2020	Trend	March 2020
Solution Quality	Data accuracy (% accuracy)	Tong	99.99%	98.82%	down	
	System Stability (%uptime)	Taurai/Nash	99.99%	99.88%	up	
	System Reliability (% issues addressed within 48 hours)	Andre	TBC	N/A	N/A	Reporting starts in June
Customer Effort	Invoice Accuracy (decrease billing inquiries by x%)	David	TBC	N/A	N/A	Reporting starts in June
	Contract Turnaround Time (# days to execute contract from 7 days to 3	Yomtej	3 days	32	Worse	22
Customer Support and Engagement	First Contact Resolution (Industry Benchmark is 70%, target is 80%)	Arun/Rowan	3 days	12	Improve	18
	Customer Communications (100% of customers receive Quarterly Newsletter)	Jamaan	100% Quarterly	100%	N/A	N/A - not sent in March

Jonathan Daniels

OPERATIONALISE

OPERATIONALISE

 DELIVER QUICK WINS

 MEASURE AND EVALUATE ROI

 EVENTS CONFIRMED

 ROLES CONFIRMED

 INPUT STRATEGY CONFIRMED

 OUTPUTS CONFIRMED

By now, you should be in a position to be able to measure and prove the profitability and positive effects of your implemented improvements. The next step is to formalise some of the processes that are working well so that these can be scaled and delivered across the organisation. To achieve this, you may want to continue to share stories of CX excellence and results to others in your organisation. You will also need to communicate the positive results and identify other allies to share the good news.

Adapt the CX CENTRIC Playbook

At this point, you can solidify how you will adapt the CX CENTRIC playbook for use in your organisation. So, you confirm the roles and responsibilities that each team member will have. Confirm the events that will take place, how often they will occur, confirm the list of invitees and send out the meeting invitations. You will confirm the outputs required and be clear on which team members will be responsible for their creation and updating the documents. And you will ensure that a strategy is in place to develop the data and information which add up to measure your customer experience.

Although at this stage, you solidify the operational aspects, keep in mind that you still need to be flexible. Be prepared for criticism and feedback and don't be scared to modify what you have created at any stage if it feels logical.

Scale across other teams

The initiation and co-creation phase will consist of one or two teams. This is often carried out to allow the leader to dig deep and focus their efforts which drives success. During the Operationalise phase, we then look to take what we have learned and transfer knowledge to other teams. Remember this should be conducted one department at a time. It is not possible to flick a switch and transform an organisation. We encourage you to list each team in your CX Horizon and have a plan for how you will engage with them, communicate with them and involve them in the plan to spread the good things you have learned from the previous two phases.

Often in large organisations, decisions and opinions are diluted. This is especially true when it comes to activities impacting customer experience. Whilst scaling a great way to ensure its success is to give people more freedom in their roles. Freedom to decide how to improve CX and then freedom to implement. By offering employees the liberty to decide and to execute impactful improvements as a team, you increase their motivation to become customer-centric.

Measure and evaluate ROI

By this time, you will have challenged KPIs and agreed on customer-centric KPIs which align both with the organisations strategy and the CX Strategy. You should also have the required inputs to not only drive customer insights, but also to measure the effectiveness of the investment decisions you have taken. Take time to review which investments led to an increase in customer satisfaction, or an increase in the customer's NPS. And take it a step further by analysing how strong the relationship is between metrics like net promoter score and number of actual referrals.

Jonathan Daniels

NOURISH

NOURISH

 DELIVER EXPERIENCE CHANGES

 RE-AUDIT

 INTRODUCE CX BEST PRACTICE

 CONTINUOUS IMPROVEMENT

At this stage, you will have already profited from many of the changes that you have introduced to your programme. However, this is not the time to let your foot off the gas. If you do not continue to prioritise CX on your company's agenda, there is a big risk that your organisation may regress back to where it started. Customer Experience is not a "one-time activity". You need to constantly deliver value and demonstrate this by positively impacting business KPIs. Your teams should always be focused on bringing growth to your business by delivering exceptional experiences that your customers appreciate and remember. By focusing on bringing growth, you ensure that Customer Experience continues to be a sustainable and profitable strategy for your business, rather than just an initiative.

TOP TIP

Customer Experience is not a "Project"

Ruth Crowley

Fortune 100 Retail Company

"The value of the ICON framework has been field-tested in small and large retail settings. Without applying the principles, prior projects failed. The research and pre-work was done and the framework was solid, but the customer-centric focus did not survive past the point of operationalisation. People just moved onto the next priority. To gain full value of the ICON model it is critical to ensure people are informed and engaged for sustainable results. Customer Experience is not a "project".

TOP TIP

Don't be afraid to test new things. Customer Experience is largely about what and how we communicate. It's OK to get things wrong as long as they don't stay wrong.

Never stop delivering

As your organisation matures, the teams will become better and better at delivering things your customers appreciate. You will receive validation of the effectiveness of your CX through contact and interaction from customers. You will also receive validation through your revenue and profits. However, in order to stay ahead of the curve and in order to continue to grow, your organisation must keep delivering improvements to the customer's journey. By focusing on offering value to the customers and by not holding back on your investments in CX, you create customers who are ambassadors for your business.

When courting a partner, there are many who start off very well in the beginning —pulling out all the stops to impress and to show that they care. This often ends in a crescendo, especially at the time of the proposal. Often, after a few years, your partner may begin to take you for granted. They don't surprise you anymore; they stop trying to work out how to please you. They think that what pleased you five years ago will please you today. So, they buy you the same sorts of presents and take you to the same restaurants. Meanwhile your interests have changed. You are not the same person you once were although you do appreciate what they did for you over the years. This is the same with your customers. Don't take them for granted. Keep the focus on the shared problem and take actions to surprise and inspire them. Show them that you care about improving their day. Otherwise, another organisation will rock on the scene and take advantage of the situation.

 **TOP TIP**

Keep on Evolving

Naeem Arif

Director of NA Consulting

If you are truly interested in growing your organisation, you will realise that if you are not evolving, then you are being left behind. At NAConsulting we take a quarterly review of our performance and we focus on our top 10 clients that we want to work with. We look to see what is changing in their industry and we then evaluate if we are able to meet their evolving needs.

By making small regular improvements to your customers' experience, this in itself becomes a source of competitive advantage. It reassures customers that you are focused on working with them to tackle the shared problem in the long run. And this helps them to stay with you and reject other businesses, even if they are offered promotions or lower prices.

Also, by continuing to empower your employees to take risks in the effort to differentiate your experience and offer something exceptional to your customers, you motivate them. You cultivate employees who care and share your mission. And you benefit from a healthy working environment where teamwork and a genuine passion for pleasing the customer coexist.

TOP TIP

Nurturing the relationship

Simone Smith

Director of Curious Pencil Ltd

When we think about the customer journey, there is often a temptation to finish mapping it at the sale. However, it is essential to remember our customers are layered human beings, who have most likely purchased based on emotion, so like any relationship, we must continue to work at it. It costs 6x more to acquire a new customer than it does to keep one, so nurturing your existing customers benefits both you and them. Therefore, it is extremely important to continue a mapped cycle of delivering great customer experience beyond the initial sale. Think about ways you can remain in contact, whether it's a scheduled call to check-in or a thank you card/gift on the anniversary of them being a customer.

As specialists in corporate greeting cards, we often see the impact a small gesture has. For example, a recruitment agency that is a client of ours, sends cards to their candidates congratulating them on getting their job. But it doesn't stop there. They also send cards 6 months after, not only to thank them but also to check in on how they are doing. This shows that they are still on their mind and that delivering great service doesn't stop just at the job placement. They have gone beyond the norm, instantly becoming more memorable to the candidates. This card impacted one of our client's candidates so much, that they reached out to express their gratitude and stated they will always recommend the recruitment agency to friends and family. Now, this same candidate has added greeting cards in the customer journey of their place of work. To be memorable, it is essential to keep delivering and think beyond the initial purchase (or job placement in this example).

Re-Audit Periodically

You carried out an audit when you initiated the transformation. Now you have managed to scale the practices, methods and processes across the organisation. Are things perfect now? No! Although you will be miles ahead in comparison to where you started, there will always be room to improve, along with genuine challenges. Hence, we recommend periodically conducting a CX Audit.

By re-conducting a CX Audit, you will be able to identify gaps, just as you did when you initiated the transformation. You can answer some key questions, such as:

- Is the CX strategy your team produced still relevant now?

- In light of the new technology available, are their experiences that customers are missing out on that could motivate them to switch to a competitor?

- How do your KPIs compare to the previous year and to the rest of the market?

- Are the movements in your KPIs reflective of the customer behaviours you have experienced?

- Has there been any movement in the CX scores since the previous audit?

By periodically conducting an audit, you will be able to evaluate the efficiency and effectiveness of your current Customer Experience governance. You can determine whether it is still supporting you to deliver your business strategy, or if it needs improving.

Continuously Introduce CX best practice

There are numerous organisations who continue to advance the subject of customer experience. These organisations share best practices, case studies, research papers and guidance, as to how we can continue to deliver stronger and increasingly differentiated experiences. An example is the Customer Experience Professionals Association (CXPA). This is a community to help CX leaders keep abreast for CX best practices/emerging ideas.

We recommend that you ensure that your organisation is 'clued-up' on the latest advancements and possibilities related to customer experience. This will allow you to pick and choose from examples arising from outside your business. Yes, it is important to take on feedback from employees and customers, but we encourage you to remain connected to experts across the industry. Many of these experts make it their job to understand the latest top tips and best practice for offering excellent experiences.

Continuously improve governance

The customer experience governance structure that you have assembled may serve you well today, but may not serve you well tomorrow. That is not to say that it was a waste of time to implement it! There are a lot of moving parts in our complex landscape today. This calls for the need for organisations to be agile. Agility does not just refer to the ability to develop new products. It also refers to how we work together. The meetings, roles, documents and processes you have established need to be developed over time. For this reason, we propose a regular retrospect where teams reflect on the current challenges and agree on actions to overcome them.

REFERENCES

BlaBlaCar - About Us
https://blog.blablacar.com/about-us

BlaBlaCar: The Member is the Boss.Listening to the community   https://blog.blablacar.com/blog/inside-story/member-is-the-boss

Coldwell, J., (2001). Characteristics of a Good Customer Satisfaction Survey. In J. N. Sheth, A. Parvatiyar and G. Shainesh, eds., Customer Relationship Management, New Delhi, Tata McGraw-Hill , 2001, pp193-199.

Customer experience management in the age of big data analytics: A strategic framework (2020). Maria Holmlund, Yves Van Vaerenbergh, Robert Ciuchita, Annika Ravald, Panagiotis Sarantopoulos, Francisco Villarroel Ordenes, Mohamed Zaki, Journal of Business Research,

The CX Playbook

https://www.sciencedirect.com/science/article/pii/S0148296320300345)

Customer-Centric Business Modeling: Setting a Research Agenda   Jürgen Moormann, Elisabeth Z. Palvölgyi   To cite this document: Moormann, J./Palvölgyi, E.Z. Customer-centric Business Modeling: Setting a Research Agenda, in: Proceedings of 2013 IEEE International Conference on Business Informatics, 15.-18.7.2013, Wien, S. 173-179, DOI: http://doi.ieeecomputersociety.org/10.1109/CBI.2013.33

Digital Transformation Is Not About Technology by Behnam Tabrizi, Ed Lam, Kirk Girard and Vernon Irvin MARCH 13, 2019 Harvard Business Review

https://bluecirclemarketing.com/wp-content/uploads/2019/07/Digital-Transformation-Is-Not-About-Technology.pdf

Enhancing Customer Engagement Through Consciousness .Dhruv Grewal, Anne L.Roggeveen, Rajendra Sisodia and Jens Nordfält) Journal of Retailing Volume 93, Issue 1, March 2017, Pages 55-64

Fain, I. (2014). "The Mask Behind the Veil: Identifying the Many-Faced Consumer Across Channels". Colloquy, April 2014.

Henderson, J.C. and J.G. Sifonis (1998). The value of strategic IS planning: Understanding consistency, validity and IS markets. MIS Quarterly 12: 187-200

Henderson, J. and Venkatraman, N. (1990). Strategic Alignment: A model fororganizational transformation

Jonathan Daniels

via information technology. Cambridge, MA:Sloan School of Management, Massachusetts Institute of Technology. WorkingPaper No. 3223-90

Huang, Xu & Iun, Joyce & Liu, Aili & Gong, Yaping. (2009). Does Participative Leadership Enhance Work Performance by Inducing Empowerment or Trust? The Differential Effects on Managerial and Non-Managerial Subordinates. Journal of Organizational Behavior. 31. 122 - 143. 10.1002/job.636.

J. P. Womack and T. J. Daniel, "Lean consumption," Harvard Business Review, vol. 83, no. 3, pp. 58-68, 2005.

Kevin McShane (2012) Customer Centricity in the Telecommunications Industry. Pitney Bowes Software, Inc.

Kilian, K. (2009) in Lindgreen, A., Beverland, M.B. and Vanhamme, J. (Eds.): Memorable Customer Experiences - A Research Anthology, Gower, Surrey, England.

Leather, D. (2014). The Challenges of Implementing Customer-Centric Strategy - What Creates the Problem? [online] Customer Think. Available at: http://customerthink.com/the-challenges-of-implementing-customer-centric-strategy-what-creates-the-problem

McLean, E., & Soden, J., (1977). Strategic Planning for MIS, New York, John Wiley & Sons.

Nielsen - Under the influence: Consumer trust in advertising 09-17-2013:https://www.nielsen.com/us/en/insights/article/2013/under-the-influence-consumer-trust-in-

166

advertising/

Organizational Strategy for World recognized organization focusing on customer, 2018 (Abdullahi Bala Ado, Kabiru Tsoho & Kuwata Goni) Available at: https://icss.nileuniversity.edu.ng/wp-content/uploads/sites/37/2020/02/Business-Admin-Proceeding-Book-2018.pdf#page=163

SPECIAL THANKS

Special thanks to my brother Saad Qureshi, who proof reads everything I do - A true wizard on the keyboard. And a very special thanks to my mum, Sandra Daniels, who taught me how to read and write.

CONTRIBUTERS

Ali Malik

Anna Noakes Schulze

Chris Turner

Diederik Proot

Errol Lawson

Eva Tzofia Moritz

Ian Golding

Janelle Mansfield

John D Hanson

Jonathan Daniels

Kerri Nelson

Mandisa Makubalo

Marilyn Daley

Momchil Blaskov

Michelle Spaul

Naeem Arif

Nyasha Maphosa

Olga Guseva

Rajeev Karkhanis

Révérien Uwacu

Ruth Crowley

Simone Smith

Sue Nabeth Moore

Tonja Pena

Yuri Vedenin

YOUR NEXT STEPS

My goal writing this book is to give practical guidance to leaders who want to develop and implement customer-centric strategies.

I hope that this content has been valuable to you. And that I have "earned the right to" become a trusted resource for you as you grow your business.

There is a vibrant community of CX CENTRIC supporters across the world. I would love you to be a part of the movement.

You can connect with me at jonathan@cx-centric.com, it would be an honour to connect with you.

ABOUT THE AUTHOR

With over a decade of experience in transforming organisations, Jonathan certainly understands the importance of customer experience. As a CCXP he has worked with an impressive portfolio of consulting clients such as Nissan, Lloyds Banking Group, ING, Visable, and Sodexo. Jonathan is also the co-author of the global bestseller: Customer Experience.

Jonathan is the author of both the CX CENTRIC playbook and the ICON process. He offers consultancy services as well as training. He is also a passionate and engaging public speaker.

Jonathan is co-founder of CX-Brussels, which exists to bring customer experience professionals across Belgium together, so they can learn, share and advance the subject of Customer Experience.

He has a Bachelor's degree in Computer Science and Business and a Masters in Programme and Project Management from the University of Warwick.

Jonathan is the oldest of four brothers. All of which are skillful musicians.

Printed in Great Britain
by Amazon

40775805R00108